New York Mets 2019

A Baseball Companion

Edited by Patrick Dubuque, Aaron Gleeman and Bret Sayre

Baseball Prospectus

Craig Brown and Dave Pease, Consultant Editors
Rob McQuown and Harry Pavlidis, Statistics Editors

Copyright © 2019 by DIY Baseball, LLC.
All rights reserved

This book or any part thereof may not be reproduced or transmitted in any form or by any means, electronic or mechanical, including photocopying, recording, or by any information storage and retrieval system, without permission in writing from the publisher.

Limit of Liability/Disclaimer of Warranty: While the publisher and the author have used their best efforts in preparing this book, they make no representations or warranties with respect to the accuracy or completeness of the contents of this book and specifically disclaim any implied warranties of merchantability or fitness for a particular purpose. No warranty may be created or extended by sales representatives or written sales materials. The advice and strategies contained herein may not be suitable for your situation. You should consult with a professional where appropriate. Neither the publisher nor the author shall be liable for any loss of profit or any other commercial damages, including but not limited to special, incidental, consequential, or other damages.

Library of Congress Cataloging-in-Publication Data:
paperback
ISBN-13: 978-1-949332-46-9

Project Credits
Cover Design: Kathleen Dyson
Interior Design and Production: Jeff Pease, Dave Pease
Layout: Jeff Pease, Dave Pease

Baseball icon courtesy of Uberux, from https://www.shareicon.net/author/uberux

Ballpark diagram courtesy of Lou Spirito/THIRTY81 Project, https://thirty81project.com/

Manufactured in the United States of America
10 9 8 7 6 5 4 3 2 1

Table of Contents

Foreword v
    Rob Mains

Statistical Introduction vii

Part 1: Team Analysis

Table for Three: Previewing the 2019 New York Mets 3
    Kate Feldman, Tyler Oringer and Jarrett Seidler

Performance Graphs 9

2018 Team Performance 10

2019 Team Projections 11

Team Personnel 12

Citi Field Stats 13

Mets Team Analysis 15

Part 2: Player Analysis

Mets Player Analysis 22

Mets Prospects 107

Part 3: Featured Articles

The Hole in The Shift is Fixing Itself 121
    Russell Carleton

The State of the Quality Start 125
    Rob Mains

Heads-Up Hacking—The First Pitch 131
    Matthew Trueblood

A Hymn for the Index Stat 137
    Patrick Dubuque

Index of Names 141

Foreword

Rob Mains

Welcome to this companion of the 2019 New York Mets. We at Baseball Prospectus are excited to provide this analysis of the Mets.

Our website, Baseball Prospectus, is a leader in delivering high-quality commentary and data to baseball fans everywhere. To some, those words—commentary and data—appear mutually exclusive. There are people out there who believe that traditional analysis and advanced analytics must run on different paths. But the simplistic narrative of stats vs. traditionalists just isn't true. Every team's analytics department interacts with scouting, development, and major league operations with a common goal: Delivering a championship. New technologies, like radar tracking of pitch speeds and movement, enable talent evaluators to focus on qualitative aspects of pitching like mechanics and pitch sequencing. In-game strategies like infield shifts, based on batters' hit tendencies, help turn balls in play into outs. Hitters use information to adjust their swings to maximize run production.

All these numbers can seem, at best, intimidating, and at worst, counterproductive to the casual fan. Even as technology and analysis have embedded themselves deeply into the way teams run, it can often feel like statistics create a displacement between the viewer and the sport, breaking them out of the action. And yet every fan incorporates the numbers to some degree; stats like batting average and earned run average, so fundamental to how we talk about performance, are actually complicated formulas. They don't bother people because those formulas have become second nature, as easy to translate as the action on the field.

Along the way, new statistics have entered baseball's lexicon. You'll see some of them, like on-base percentage (which measures a batter's ability to get on base via walk, hit batter, or hit), OPS (on-base plus slugging), and average exit velocity (the speed of balls off a hitter's bat) on broadcasts. Others, like DRC+, might well be new to you. Some of them have been well-defined to the public, others haven't. That lack of context has created ambiguity. Fans know that a ball hit 100 mph is scorched, but does that mean extra bases? (Not if it's hit on the ground or high in the air it doesn't.)

For those who are amenable to them, the new statistics can increase the enjoyment and understanding of the game. They can help fans identify when a pitcher is tiring, when a stolen base or a bunt attempt makes sense (and, more often, when it doesn't), or how a team's lineup might be constructed. Websites like Baseball Prospectus add to that understanding by weaving metrics into the narrative of the game. That's the goal of this publication: to take some of the newer, more complicated statistics and make them as intuitive as the ones on the back of old baseball cards.

But you don't need to love analytics to love baseball. The fans at BP who worked together to write this guide are captivated first and foremost by the game itself. We're drawn to Aaron Judge's power, Francisco Lindor's glove, Billy Hamilton's speed and Patrick Corbin's slider and don't need numbers to tell us why they're so mesmerizing. The underlying statistics provide depth to the game that we all love.

We hope you'll find that this guide helps you better understand the Mets. Our analysts have studied the team's major league personnel and its minor league affiliates to identify their strengths and weaknesses, both the obvious ones and those that only a careful dissection of players' performances—yes, including the data—can reveal. You don't need us to tell you who was good and who wasn't in 2018, but our models and writers can help you project how each player is going to perform this year and beyond, and appreciate the greatness of each new game as it unfolds. As in the sport itself, the human and analytic components combine to generate a deeper overall understanding.

Think back to the first time you saw a baseball game on a high-definition TV. You'd grown familiar with how the game looked and felt on a picture tube. But new TV allowed you to see details that you'd never seen before. That's how advanced statistics work. The game itself is why you're here and why you're buying this. (And, for that matter, why we wrote it.) The statistical measures provide the sharper focus, the detail, the depth of knowledge that you didn't have before, generating an overall superior picture. Enjoy the view.

—*Rob Mains is an author of Baseball Prospectus.*

Statistical Introduction

Sports are, fundamentally, a blend of athletic endeavor and storytelling. Baseball, like any other sport, tells its stories in so many ways: in the arc of a game from the stands or a season from the box scores, in photos, or even in numbers. At Baseball Prospectus, we understand that statistics don't replace observation or any of baseball's stories, but complement everything else that makes the game so much fun.

What stats help us with is with patterns and precision, variance and value. This book can help you learn things you may not see from watching a game or hundred, whether it's the path of a career over time or the breadth of the entire MLB. We'd also never ask you to choose between our numbers and the experience of viewing a game from the cheap seats or the comfort of your home; our publication combines running the numbers with observations and wisdom from some of the brightest minds we can find. But if you *do* want to learn more about the numbers beyond what's on the backs of player jerseys, let us help explain.

Offense

At the end of this past year, we've revised our methodology for determining batting value. Long-time readers of Baseball Prospectus will notice that we've retired True Average in favor of a new metric: Deserved Runs Created Plus (DRC+). Developed by Jonathan Judge and our stats team, this statistic measures everything a player does at the plate–reaching base, hitting for power, making outs, and moving runners over–and puts it on a scale where 100 equals league-average performance. A DRC+ of 150 is terrific, a DRC+ of 100 is average, and a DRC+ of 75 means you better be an excellent defender.

DRC+ also does a better job than any of our previous metrics in taking contextual factors into account. The model adjusts for how the park affects performance, but also for things like the talent of the opposing pitcher, value of different types of batted-ball events, league, temperature, and other factors. It's able to describe a player's expected offensive contribution than any other statistic we've found over the years, and also does a better job of predicting future performance as well.

The other aspect of run-scoring is baserunning, which we quantify using Baserunning Runs. BRR not only records the value of stolen bases (or getting caught in the act), but also accounts for a runner's ability to go first to third on a single or advance on a fly ball.

Defense

Where offensive value is *relatively* easy to identify and understand, defensive value is ... not. Over the past dozen years, the sabermetric community has focused mostly on stats based on zone data: a real-live human person records the type of batted ball and estimated landing location, and models are created that give expected outs. From there, you can compare fielders' actual outs to those expected ones. Simple, right?

Unfortunately, zone data has two major issues. First, zone data is recorded by commercial data providers who keep the raw data private unless you pay for it. (All the statistics we build in this book and on our website use public data as inputs.) That hurts our ability to test assumptions or duplicate results. Second, over the years it has become apparent that there's quite a bit of "noise" in zone-based fielding analysis. Sometimes the conclusions drawn from zone data don't hold up to scrutiny, and sometimes the different data provided by different providers don't look anything alike, giving wildly different results. Sometimes the hard-working professional stringers or scorers might unknowingly inflict unconscious bias into the mix: for example good fielders will often be credited with more expected outs despite the data, and ballparks with high press boxes tend to score more line drives than ones with a lower press box.

Enter our Fielding Runs Above Average (FRAA). For most positions, FRAA is built from play-by-play data, which allows us to avoid the subjectivity found in many other fielding metrics. The idea is this: count how many fielding plays are made by a given player and compare that to expected plays for an average fielder at their position (based on pitcher ground-ball tendencies and batter handedness). Then we adjust for park and base-out situations.

When it comes to catchers, our methodology is a little different thanks to the laundry list of responsibilities they're tasked with beyond just, well, catching and throwing the ball. By now you've probably heard about "framing" or the art of making umpires more likely to call balls outside the strike zone for strikes. To put this into one tidy number, we incorporate pitch tracking data (for the years it exists) and adjust for important factors like pitcher, umpire, batter, and home-field advantage using a mixed-model approach. This grants us a number for how many strikes the catcher is personally adding to (or subtracting from) his pitchers' performance ... which we then convert to runs added or lost using linear weights.

Framing is one of the biggest parts of determining catcher value, but we also take into account blocking balls from going past, whether a scorer deems it a passed ball or a wild pitch. We use a similar approach–one that really benefits from the pitch tracking data that tells us what ends up in the dirt and what doesn't. We also include a catcher's ability to prevent stolen bases and how well they field balls in play, and *finally* we come up with our FRAA for catchers.

Pitching

Both pitching and fielding make up the half of baseball that isn't run scoring: run prevention. Separating pitching from fielding is a tough task, and most recent pitching analysis has branched off from Voros McCracken's famous (and controversial) statement, "There is little if any difference among major-league pitchers in their ability to prevent hits on balls hit in the field of play." The research of the analytic community has validated this to some extent, and there are a host of "defense-independent" pitching measures that have been developed to try and extricate the effect of the defense behind a hurler from the pitcher's work.

Our solution to this quandry is Deserved Run Average (DRA), our core pitching metric. DRA looks like earned run average (ERA), the tried-and-true pitching stat you've seen on every baseball broadcast or box score from the past century, but it's very different. To start, DRA takes an event-by-event look at what the pitchers does, and adjusts the value of that event based on different environmental factors like park, batter, catcher, umpire, base-out situation, run differential, inning, defense, home field advantage, pitcher role, and temperature. That mixed model gives us a pitcher's expected contribution, similar to what we do for our DRC+ model for hitters and FRAA model for catchers. (Oh, and we also consider the pitcher's effect on basestealing and on balls getting past the catcher.)

It's important to note that DRA is set to the scale of runs allowed per nine innings (RA9) instead of ERA, which makes DRA's scale slightly higher than ERA's. The reason for this is because ERA tends to overrate three types of pitchers:

1. Pitchers who play in parks where scorers hand out more errors. Official scorers differ significantly in the frequency at which they assign errors to fielders.
2. Ground-ball pitchers, because a substantial proportion of errors occur on grounders.
3. Pitchers who aren't very good. Better pitchers often allow fewer unearned runs than bad pitchers, because good pitchers tend to find ways to get out of jams.

Since the last time you picked up an edition of this book, we've also made a few minor changes to DRA to make it better. Recent research into "tunneling"–the act of throwing consecutive pitches that appear similar from a batter's point of view until after the swing decision point–data has given us a new contextual factor to account for in DRA: plate distance. This refers to the distance between successive pitches as they approach the plate, and while it has a smaller effect than factors like velocity or whiff rate, it still can help explain pitcher strikeout rate in our model.

New Pitching Metrics for 2019

We're including a few "new" pitching metrics for 2019's suite of Baseball Prospectus publications, but you may be familiar with them if you've spent time scouring the internet for stats.

Fastball Percentage

Our fastball percentage (FB%) statistic measures how frequently a pitcher throws a pitch classified as a "fastball," measured as a percentage of overall pitches thrown. We qualify three types of fastballs:

1. The traditional four-seam fastball;
2. The two-seam fastball or sinker;
3. "Hard cutters," which are pitches that have the movement profile of a cut fastball and are used as the pitcher's primary offering or in place of a more traditional fastball.

For example, a pitcher with a FB% of 67 throws any combination of these three pitches about two-thirds of the time.

Whiff Rate

Everybody loves a swing and a miss, and whiff rate (WHF) measures how frequently pitchers induce a swinging strike. To calculate WHF, we add up all the pitches thrown that ended with a swinging strike, then divide that number by a pitcher's total pitches thrown. Most often, high whiff rates correlate with high strikeout rates (and overall effective pitcher performance).

Called Strike Probability

Called Strike Probability (CSP) is a number that represents the likelihood that all of a pitcher's pitches will be called a strike while controlling for location, pitcher and batter handedness, umpire and count. Here's how it works: on each pitch, our model determines how many times (out of 100) that a similar pitch was called for a strike given those factors mentioned above, and when normalized for each batter's strike zone. Then we average the CSP for all pitches thrown by a pitcher in a season, and that gives us the yearly CSP percentage you see in the stats boxes.

As you might imagine, pitchers with a higher CSP are more likely to work in the zone, where pitchers with a lower CSP are likely locating their pitches outside the normal strike zone, for better or for worse.

Projections

Many of you aren't turning to this book just for a look at what a player has done, but for a look at what a player is going to do: the PECOTA projections. PECOTA, initially developed by Nate Silver (who has moved on to greater fame as a political analyst), consists of three parts:

1. Major-league equivalencies, which use minor-league statistics to project how a player will perform in the major leagues;
2. Baseline forecasts, which use weighted averages and regression to the mean to estimate a player's current true talent level; and
3. Aging curves, which uses the career paths of comparable players to estimate how a player's statistics are likely to change over time.

With all those important things covered, let's take a look at what's in the book this year.

Team Prospectus

You bought this book to learn more about your favorite (or maybe least-favorite, who are we to judge?) team, so let's talk about them. After a thoughtful preview of the 2019 season, you'll be presented with our Team Prospectus. This outlines many of the key statistics for each team's 2018 season, as well as a very inviting stadium diagram.

First you'll find the Performance Graphs page. The first is the 2018 Hit List Ranking. This shows our Hit List Rank for the team on each day of the 2018 season and is intended to give you a picture of the ups and downs of the team's season, including their highest and lowest ranks of the year. Hit List Rank measures overall team performance and drives the Hit List Power Rankings at the baseballprospectus.com website.

The second graph is Committed Payroll and helps you see how the team's payroll has compared to the MLB and divisional average payrolls over time. Payroll figures are currents as of January 1, 2019; with so many free agents still unsigned as of this writing, the final 2018 figure will likely be significantly different for many teams. (In the meantime, you can always find the most current data at Baseball Prospectus' Cot's Baseball Contracts page.)

The third graph is Farm System Ranking and displays how the Baseball Prospectus prospect team has ranked the organization's farm system since 2007. It also indicates the highest and lowest ranks that the farm system achieved over that time.

We start the Team Performance page with the squad's unadjusted and third-order 2018 win-loss records, presented in divisional context. We then list the three highest performing hitters and pitchers by WARP for 2018. Beneath that are a host of other team statistics. **Pythag** presents an adjusted 2018 winning percentage, calculated by taking runs scored per game (**RS/G**) and runs allowed per game (**RA/G**) for the team, and running them through a version of Bill James' Pythagorean formula that was refined and improved by David Smyth and Brandon Heipp. (The formula is called "Pythagenpat," which is equally fun to type and to say.)

Next up is **DRC+**, described earlier, to indicate the overall hitting ability of the team either above or below league-average. Run prevention on the pitching side is covered by **DRA** (also mentioned earlier) and another metric: Fielding Independent Pitching (**FIP**), which calculates another ERA-like statistic based on strikeouts, walks, and home runs recorded. Defensive Efficiency Rating (**DER**) tells us the percentage of balls in play turned into outs for the team, and is a quick fielding shorthand that rounds out run prevention.

After that, we have several measures related to roster composition, as opposed to on-field performance. **B-Age** and **P-Age** tell us the average age of a team's batters and pitchers, respectively. **Salary** is the combined team payroll for all on-field players, and Doug Pappas' Marginal Dollars per Marginal Win (**M$/MW**) tells us how much money a team spent to earn production above replacement level.

Ending this batch of statistics is the number of disabled list days a team had over the season (**DL Days**) and the amount of salary paid to players on the disabled list (**$ on DL**); this final number is expressed as a percentage of total payroll.

Next to each of these stats, we've listed each team's MLB rank in that category from 1st to 30th. In this, 1st always indicates a positive outcome and 30th a negative outcome, except in the case of salary–1st is highest.

The Team Projections page is intended to convey the team's operational capacity entering the 2019 season. We start with the team's PECOTA projected record for 2019, again in divisional context. The **+/-** column indicates how many more or less wins the team is projected to get than they got in 2018. We then list the three highest projected hitters and pitchers by WARP for 2018. A brief farm system summary follows, with the team's top prospect and number of BP Top 101 Prospects. Finally, we list the key new players and departed players, along with their 2019 projected WARP.

Alex Bregman 3B

Born: 03/30/94   Age: 25   Bats: R   Throws: R
Height: 6'0"   Weight: 180   Origin: Round 1, 2015 Draft (#2 overall)

YEAR	TEAM	LVL	AGE	PA	R	2B	3B	HR	RBI	BB	K	SB	CS	AVG/OBP/SLG
2016	CCH	AA	22	285	54	16	2	14	46	42	26	5	3	.297/.415/.559
2016	FRE	AAA	22	83	17	6	0	6	15	5	12	2	1	.333/.373/.641
2016	HOU	MLB	22	217	31	13	3	8	34	15	52	2	0	.264/.313/.478
2017	HOU	MLB	23	626	88	39	5	19	71	55	97	17	5	.284/.352/.475
2018	HOU	MLB	24	705	105	51	1	31	103	96	85	10	4	.286/.394/.532
2019	HOU	MLB	25	675	96	38	3	23	78	73	107	12	4	.272/.359/.463

Breakout: 6%   Improve: 52%   Collapse: 5%   Attrition: 2%   MLB: 100%
Comparables: Anthony Rendon, David Wright, Pablo Sandoval

YEAR	TEAM	LVL	AGE	PA	DRC+	VORP	BABIP	BRR	FRAA	WARP
2016	CCH	AA	22	285	172	38.9	.286	1.6	SS(51): -3.4, 3B(11): 1.4	2.7
2016	FRE	AAA	22	83	161	10.0	.333	-1.2	SS(14): 2.1, LF(3): -0.1	0.8
2016	HOU	MLB	22	217	107	9.6	.317	0.5	3B(40): 0.9, SS(5): -0.1	1.1
2017	HOU	MLB	23	626	114	34.7	.311	-1.5	3B(132): 8.7, SS(30): -2.9	3.9
2018	HOU	MLB	24	705	150	72.6	.289	-1.6	3B(136): 5.4, SS(28): -0.4	7.4
2019	HOU	MLB	25	675	125	37.3	.295	0.0	3B 7, SS 0	4.6

After the projections page, we share a few items about the team's home ballpark. There's the aforementioned diagram of the park's dimensions (including distances to the outfield wall), a few important biographical facts about the stadium, a graphic showing the height of the wall from the left-field pole to the right-field pole, and a table showing three-year park factors for the stadium. The park factors are displayed as indexes where 100 is average, 110 means that the park inflates the statistic in question by 10 percent, and 90 means that the park deflates the statistic in question by 10 percent.

Following the ballpark page, we have a **Personnel** section that lists many of the important decision-makers and upper-level field and operations staff members for the franchise, as well as any former Baseball Prospectus staff members who are currently part of the organization.

Position Players

After all that information and a thoughtful bylined essay covering each team, we present our player comments. Each player is listed with the major-league team who employed him as of early January 2019. If a player changed teams after that point via free agency, trade, or any other method, you'll be able to find them in the book for their previous squad.

First, we cover biographical information (age is as of June 30, 2019) before moving onto the stats themselves. Our statistic columns include standard identifying information like **YEAR**, **TEAM**, **LVL** (level of affiliated play) and **AGE** before getting into the numbers. Next, we provide raw, unstranslated numbers like you might find on the back of your dad's baseball cards: **PA** (plate appearances), **R** (runs), **2B** (doubles), **3B** (triples), **HR** (home runs), **RBI** (runs batted in), **BB** (walks), **K** (strikeouts), **SB** (stolen bases) and **CS** (caught stealing). Then we have unadjusted "slash" statistics: **AVG** (batting average), **OBP** (on-base percentage) and **SLG** (slugging percentage).

Just below the stats box is **PECOTA** data, which is discussed further in a following section. After that, it's on to a pithy and always-informative comment written by a member of the Baseball Prospectus staff, before we cover more stats.

The second text box repeats YEAR, TEAM, LVL, AGE, and PA, then moves on to **DRC+** (Deserved Runs Created Plus), which we described earlier as total offensive expected contribution compared to the league average. Next, one of our oldest active metrics, **VORP** (Value Over Replacement Player), considers offensive production, position and plate appearances. In essence, it is the number of runs contributed beyond what a replacement-level player at the same position would contribute if given the same percentage of team plate appearances. VORP does not consider the quality of a player's defense.

BABIP (batting average on balls in play) tells us how often a ball in play fell for a hit, and can help us identify whether a batter may have been lucky or not … but note that high BABIPs also tend to follow the great hitters of our time, as well as speedy singles hitters who put the ball on the ground.

The next item is **BRR** (Baserunning Runs), which covers all of a player's baserunning accomplishments which includes (but isn't limited to) swiped bags and failed attempts. Next is **FRAA** (Fielding Runs Above Average), which also includes the number of games previously played at each position noted in parentheses. Multi-position players have only their two most frequent positions listed here, but their total FRAA number reflects all positions played.

Our last column here is **WARP** (Wins Above Replacement Player). WARP estimates the total value of a player, which means for hitters it takes into account hitting runs above average (calculated using the DRC+ model), BRR and FRAA. Then, it makes an adjustment for positions played and gives the player a credit for plate appearances based upon the difference between "replacement level"¬–which is derived from the quality of players added to a team's roster after the start of the season¬–and the league average.

Catchers

Catchers are a special breed, and thus they have earned their own separate box which displays some of the defensive metrics that we've built just for them. As an example, let's check out J.T. Realmuto.

YEAR	TEAM	P. COUNT	FRM RUNS	BLK RUNS	THRW RUNS	TOT RUNS
2016	MIA	18935	-8.5	1.8	2.1	-5.6
2017	MIA	18959	5.3	1.7	1.0	9.1
2018	MIA	16399	-0.4	0.9	0.1	0.4
2019	PHI	18448	-1.4	1.5	0.7	0.8

The **YEAR** and **TEAM** columns match what you'd find in the other stat box. **P. COUNT** indicates the number of pitches thrown while the catcher was behind the plate, including swinging strikes, fouls, and balls in play. **FRM RUNS** is the total run value the catcher provided (or cost) his team by influencing the umpire to call strikes where other catchers did not. **BLK RUNS** expresses the total run value above or below average for the catcher's ability to prevent wild pitches and passed balls. **THRW RUNS** is calculated using a similar model as the previous two statistics, and it measures a catcher's ability to throw out basestealers but also to dissuade them from testing his arm in the first place. It takes into account factors like the pitcher (including his delivery and pickoff move) and baserunner (who could be as fast as Billy Hamilton or as slow as Yonder Alonso). **TOT RUNS** is the sum of all of the previous three statistics.

Pitchers

Let's give our pitchers a turn, using 2018 NL Cy Young winner Jacob deGrom as our example. Take a look at his first stat block: the first line and the **YEAR**, **TEAM**, **LVL** and **AGE** columns are the same as in the position player example earlier.

Here too, we have a series of columns that display raw, unadjusted statistics compiled by the pitcher over the course of a season: **W** (wins), **L** (losses), **SV** (saves), **G** (games pitched), **GS** (games started), **IP** (innings pitched), **H** (hits allowed) and **HR** (home runs allowed). Next we have two statistics that are rates: **BB/9** (walks per nine innings) and **K/9** (strikeouts per nine innings), before returning to the unadjusted **K** (strikeouts).

Next up is **GB%** (ground ball percentage), which is the percentage of all batted balls that were hit in the ground, including both outs and hits. Remember, this is based on observational data and subject to human error, so please approach this with a healthy dose of skepticism.

BABIP (batting average on balls in play) is calculated using the same methodology as it is for position players, but it often tells us more about a pitcher than it does a hitter. With pitchers, a high BABIP is often due to poor defense or bad luck, and can often be an indicator of potential rebound, and a low BABIP may be cause to expect performance regression. (A typical league-average BABIP is close to .290-.300.)

After a witty 150ish words on the player like only Baseball Prospectus's staff can provide, it's on to that second stat block, which repeats the YEAR, TEAM, LVL, and AGE columns. The metrics **WHIP** (walks plus hits per inning pitched) and **ERA**

New York Mets 2019

(earned run average) are old standbys: WHIP measures walks and hits allowed on a per-inning basis, while ERA measures earned runs on a nine-inning basis. Neither of these stats are translated or adjusted.

DRA (Deserved Run Average) was described at length earlier, and measures how many runs the pitcher "deserved" to allow per nine innings. Please note that since we lack all the data points that would make for a "real" DRA for minor-league events, the DRA displayed for minor league partial-seasons is based off of different data. (That data is a modified version of our cFIP metric, which you can find more information about on our website.)

Jacob deGrom   RHP
Born: 06/19/88   Age: 31   Bats: L   Throws: R
Height: 6'4"   Weight: 180   Origin: Round 9, 2010 Draft (#272 overall)

YEAR	TEAM	LVL	AGE	W	L	SV	G	GS	IP	H	HR	BB/9	K/9	K	GB%	BABIP
2016	NYN	MLB	28	7	8	0	24	24	148	142	15	2.2	8.7	143	47%	.312
2017	NYN	MLB	29	15	10	0	31	31	201^1	180	28	2.6	10.7	239	48%	.305
2018	NYN	MLB	30	10	9	0	32	32	217	152	10	1.9	11.2	269	48%	.281
2019	NYN	MLB	31	13	9	0	31	31	186	145	18	2.3	10.7	221	46%	.286

Breakout: 8%   Improve: 29%   Collapse: 28%   Attrition: 6%   MLB: 85%
Comparables: Erik Bedard, A.J. Burnett, CC Sabathia

YEAR	TEAM	LVL	AGE	WHIP	ERA	DRA	WARP	MPH	FB%	WHF	CSP
2016	NYN	MLB	28	1.20	3.04	3.30	3.5	96.3	59.6	12.1	47.2
2017	NYN	MLB	29	1.19	3.53	3.02	5.7	97.2	55.5	14.5	49.5
2018	NYN	MLB	30	0.91	1.70	2.09	8.0	98.2	52.1	16.3	48.4
2019	NYN	MLB	31	1.02	2.91	3.23	3.9	96.6	54.5	14.8	48.2

Just like with hitters, **WARP** (Wins Above Replacement Player) is a total value metric that puts pitchers of all stripes on the same scale as position players. We use DRA as the primary input for our calculation of WARP. You might notice that relief pitchers (due to their limited innings) may have a lower WARP than you were expecting or than you might see in other WARP-like metrics. WARP does not take leverage into account, just the actions a pitcher performs and the expected value of those actions ... which ends up judging high-leverage relief pitchers differently than you might imagine given their prestige and market value.

MPH gives you the pitcher's 95th percentile velocity for the noted season, in order to give you an idea of what the *peak* fastball velocity a pitcher possesses. Since this comes from our pitch tracking data, it is not publicly available for minor-league pitchers.

Finally, we display the three new pitching metrics we described earlier. **FB%** (fastball percentage) gives you the percentage of fastballs thrown out of all pitches. **WhiffRt** (whiff rate) tells you the percentage of swinging strikes induced out of all pitches. **CS Prob** (called strike probability) expresses the likelihood of all pitches thrown to result in a called strike, after controlling for factors like handedness, umpire, pitch type, count, and location.

PECOTA

All players have PECOTA projections for 2019, as well as a set of other numbers that describe the performance of comparable players according to PECOTA. All projections for 2019 are for the player at the date we went to press in early January and are projected into the league and park context as indicated by the team abbreviation. All PECOTA projected statistics represent a player's projected major-league performance.

The numbers beneath the player's stats–Breakout, Improve, Collapse, Attrition–are part and parcel of the PECOTA projections. They estimate the likelihood of changes in performance relative to the player's previously-established level of production, based on the performance of comparable players:

Breakout Rate is the percent change that a player's production will improve by at least 20 percent relative to the weighted average of his performance over his most recent seasons.

Improve Rate is the percent chance that a player's production will improve at all relative to his baseline performance. A player who is expected to perform just the same as he has in the recent past will have an Improve Rate of 50 percent.

Collapse Rate is the percent chance that a position player's production will decline by at least 25 percent relative to his baseline performance.

Attrition Rate operates on playing time rather than performance. Specifically, it measures the likelihood that a player's playing time will decrease by at least 50 percent relative to his established level.

Breakout Rate and Collapse Rate can sometimes be counterintuitive for players who have already experienced a radical change in performance level. It's also worth noting that the projected decline in a player's rate performances might not be indicative of an expected decline in underlying ability or skill, but could just be an anticipated correction following a breakout season.

MLB% is the percentage of similar players who played in the major leagues in their relevant season.

The final pieces of information are the player's three highest-scoring comparable players as determined by PECOTA. All comparables represent a snapshot of how the listed player was performing at the same age as the current player, so if a 23-year-old pitcher is compared to Bartolo Colon, he's actually being compared to a 23-year-old Colon, not the version that pitched for the Rangers in 2018, nor to Colon's career as a whole.

A few points about pitcher projections. First, we aren't yet projecting peak velocity, so that column will be blank in the PECOTA lines. Second, projecting DRA is trickier than evaluating past performance, because it is unclear how deserving each pitcher will be of his anticipated outcomes. However, we know that another DRA-related statistic–contextual FIP or cFIP–estimates future run scoring very well. So for PECOTA, the projected DRA figures you see are based on the past cFIPs generated by the pitcher and comparable players over time, along with the other factors described above.

Lineouts

In each chapter's Lineouts section, you'll find abbreviated text comments, as well as most of same information you'd find in our full player comments. We limit the stats boxes in this section to only including the 2018 information for each player.

Exclusive Player Visualizations

In our constant battle to provide you with new and interesting baseball content you can't find anywhere else, we've added a trio of data visualizations to each hitter's entry in these books and a pair of visualizations for each pitcher.

For hitters, you'll find three new infographics. The first is each player's **Batted Ball Distribution**, which displays the five major sections of the field: LF (left), LCF (left center), CF (center), RCF (right center), and RF (right). The percentage indicated tells us what percentage of batted balls from that hitter fell within that part of the field during the 2018 season. We've also included the hitter's slugging percentage on balls in play (also called **SLGCON**) for that part of the field.

You'll also see two heatmaps: **Strike Zone vs LHP** and **Strike Zone vs RHP**. These heat maps represent a view of the strike zone from behind the catcher. Areas where there is a darker coloration represent the places where a higher percentage of pitches resulted in hits. In other words, the heatmap represents a hitter's "sweet spots" for getting hits against either left-handed or right-handed pitchers, depending on the image.

Pitchers get two images that help explain what their pitches look like from a hitter's perspective: **Pitch Shape vs LHH** and **Pitch Shape vs RHH**. These images show you the shape and the "tunneling" effect of each pitcher's offerings from the batter's perspective. For each type of pitch that a pitcher throws (represented by an indicator shape), there's a set of dots indicating the flight path, where each dot represents a 0.01-second interval. This maps the average trajectory and speed of an offering, ending where the ball crosses the plate. The solid black box represents the regular strike zone, while the gray contour lines indicate the range of locations that a pitcher typically works in.

Below the image, we provide a bit more detailed information about each pitcher's average offering in the **Pitch Types** box. Here, we also list each of the pitcher's major offerings under the **Type** column.

- **Fastballs** (which usually refers to the four-seam variation)
- **Sinkers** and/or two-seam fastballs
- **Cutters** (which could include "hard" cutters like cut fastballs and "soft" cutters that resemble hard sliders)
- **Changeups** (not including most splitters)
- **Splitters** (split-fingered pitches, forkballs, and some split-changes)
- **Sliders** and/or slurves
- **Curveballs** (including spike-curveballs and knuckle-curveballs, as well as some slurvy curves)
- **Slow curveballs** and/or eephus pitches
- **Knuckleballs**
- **Screwballs**

The **Freq** column indicates the percentage of overall pitches that fall into each of those type categories; if a pitcher has a 16.55% score for changeups, then that's the percent of all pitches that he throws as changeups. **Velo** is exactly what you think it is: the average miles per hour for each pitch type. **H Mov** is the number of inches of horizontal movement on the average pitch of that type, while **V Mov** is the number of inches of vertical movement on the average pitch of that type. (At Baseball Prospectus, we measure this over the long flight of the ball and include gravity into the V Mov number in order to give you the most realistic representation of what the pitch *actually* does.)

If you're wondering about the second number in brackets, that's the index for that velocity or movement compared to the league average. Like DRC+, a score of 100 means that the speed or movement is about the same as league average, while a higher score means that there's higher velocity or movement than the league average. Numbers below 100 indicate less velocity or movement than the league average.

Part 1: Team Analysis

Table for Three: Previewing the 2019 New York Mets

Kate Feldman, Tyler Oringer and Jarrett Seidler

What player do you see collapsing in 2019?

KATE FELDMAN: Zack Wheeler terrifies me. He has been both good and healthy for one (1) season and he's coming into 2019 as the No. 3 pitcher. PECOTA has him throwing 160 innings and a 4.40 DRA, which is significantly worse than his 2018 and significantly better than the year before. He's probably in the middle of all of these numbers, and that's a perfectly fine pitcher, but if his true talent is actually his 2017 0.3 WARP, there's no one waiting to step up and fill those shoes. So it's not so much that I'm scared of Wheeler collapsing; it's that I'm scared that Wheeler is what we thought he was.

JARRETT SEIDLER: I don't see an obvious outright collapse other than Wheeler, but Wilson Ramos has substantial negative risk in career arc. He just had arguably his best offensive season as a 30-year-old catcher coming off major knee surgery. There are logical reasons for his unusual late offensive surge: 2016 Lasik surgery, frequent rest, the oddball nature of catcher career arcs. Still, he's now a 31-year-old catcher with knee problems on a team without a DH slot. Even though they should have the depth with Travis d'Arnaud and Devin Mesoraco to manage the playing time here pretty aggressively, they haven't done well presented with similar situations in the past, as recently as last year with Yoenis Cespedes. Betting on another season with a DRC+ over 120 is probably lofty.

Of course, the Mets paid Ramos like he'd already collapsed anyway, so…

TYLER ORINGER: Wheeler has the most collapse potential of any Mets player after such an impressive 2018 second half, but it is Steven Matz who comes in a close second. First, I must clarify that this isn't necessarily a collapse of 5.00 ERA proportions, but not on par with PECOTA.

PECOTA is quite high on Matz, projecting a 3.44 ERA and 3.87 DRA. Following a very productive first-half, he dropped off in July and August ballooning to a 4.60 ERA by August 16th. Now, of course this is entirely due to injuries and Matz eventually finished the year incredibly strong. But after elbow surgery in 2017 and a flexor pronator strain in his left forearm in 2018, it's wishful thinking to believe his arm will hold up enough to put up a 26-start 3.44 ERA season.

His dominant September is quite promising, but his injuries and 25 home runs allowed in 154 innings pitched leave reason to be concerned. This not a true potential collapse, but a clear regression due to ailments.

How will this team be improved by the end of the year, through trade or call-ups, compared to their roster now?

JARRETT: The Mets have one of the most obvious early-season call-ups in the game in Pete Alonso. In any rational world, Alonso would've been up last summer, and the Mets have been talking up his ability to make the roster out of spring. I think that stands a good chance to be a red herring and they're going to manipulate his service time anyway, because they've also been talking up J.D. Davis as a first base option, and they're going to need to find time for Todd Frazier and Jeff McNeil somewhere until injuries strike. Leaving first base unoccupied for a few weeks or months while Alonso "works on his defense" serves a lot of goals.

Further down, Andres Gimenez could be a factor in the second half if they need him to be. Once a prospect has had success at Double-A, he's in the MLB picture. Gimenez already held serve there in 2018. With the acquisitions of Cano and Lowrie, it's far less likely that they make such a move out of necessity, but I could see scenarios where Amed Rosario gets hurt or continues to scuffle and Gimenez becomes the choice over Luis Guillorme or a trade option.

The Mets have historically been active buyers when remotely close to contention at the deadline. The organization believes in creating "flexibility" for deadline acquisitions, and I see little reason to believe that will change under the new regime.

KATE: They've also been relatively lucky recently in those midseason acquisitions (we don't talk enough about Matt Den Dekker for Jerry Blevins), but there isn't a whole lot of talent left for them to trade from. Brodie's been successful so far and I think you're right in that this will still be the M.O., but I just hate the idea of playing out the first half and then hoping Yoenis Cespedes 2.0 is available. I guess that's baseball though.

TYLER: I think it's hard to say how this team will approach in-season trades simply due to the fact that the front office is completely new. BVW has shown a welcomed activeness as a general manager, but has also signed guys like Rajai Davis and Gregor Blanco to minor league deals. While this depth is appreciated—it remains to be seen if they will be the first choice to replace guys if injuries strike the outfield. Like Kate said, I think for the first half it makes sense to feel out the outfield with who they have now and then—if in contention—make the 2015 Cespedes move if need be rather than using organizational depth following July 31.

As for the exciting call-up. Alonso doesn't really count as he should be on the major league roster already, but that's neither here nor there. But like Jarrett said before, it isn't the worst thing in the world (also far from the best) to let the raking first baseman to get two more weeks to "work on his defense" to feel out how the infield depth will work moving forward.

In a more rational situation, I do believe this middle infield depth is very beneficial to one Andres Gimenez. Just 20 years old, there is really no reason to rush him up this season unless Rosario goes down—and even if—it looks like the Mets will get Lowrie some reps at shortstop this year. While he's already shown he could probably play in the majors this year, a bit more development between Double-A and Triple-A could set the Mets up for an intriguing 2020 for Gimenez.

How did the team approach the offseason, and did they do well given their aims?

KATE: So the main issue for me, and I think a lot of people, is that they started the offseason with SUCH big moves. Robinson Cano! Edwin Diaz! Wilson Ramos! Hell, even Brodie Van Wagenen (yes, I too look up how to spell his last name). Big, great moves. But then they just kind of gave up. They added some positional depth with Jed Lowrie and J.D. Davis, but Manny Machado was sitting right there. They brought back Jeurys Familia and signed Justin Wilson, but Craig Kimbrel is still a free agent. And you could easily copy and paste that into literally every team preview we do at BP, but the Mets started out so splashy and then forgot to finish the project.

JARRETT: It's a great offseason… as long as you ignore Harper and Machado were free agents. They did a lot of interesting things, and played market conditions well by snagging high-quality players for way less than they "should" have gone for in both trade and free agency. PECOTA sees Diaz as the best pitcher per inning in the world, the type of guy you really can't get. The Mets stepped in to combine Seattle's desire to dump some of the Cano's contract and Cano's no-trade rights to pry away a guy they wouldn't have been able to get otherwise. Lowrie and Ramos come with age/injury risk, but they only paid for marginal starter production, and those guys have been way better than that and project to continue to be.

Yet the big upgrades were out there. Harper and Machado are perfect fits for a mid-level spender with few long-term commitments that is seeking to establish a perpetual contender without an elite farm system. Ultimately, it's not just that they didn't get them, either. It's that they didn't even try, that they weren't even options.

KATE: At this point, I'm honestly more sold on them needing Dallas Keuchel (remember him? Is he even still playing baseball?) than Machado because their No. 6 starter right now is… Walker Lockett? Seth Lugo? Chris Flexen?

TYLER: Well, in terms of approach, Mets fans have to be happy with the aggressive attitude BVW undertook. So many years, players would just float around seemingly perfect for the Mets but would get overlooked due to their contract requests. I do think that the Mets are still a good (maybe elite) bat away from being a legitimate team in a very competitive NL East.

Listen, Robinson Cano is obviously still a very good baseball player and in 80 games he accumulated a 125 DRC+ last season. Edwin Diaz is a gold standard closer. And while Jed Lowrie was a solid signing and Wilson Ramos was exactly what they needed for the dollar amount they spent, there are two people mentioned above who could be catapult the Mets into NL East Championship contention if the Mets decided to. Lowrie is good, McNeil is good, Cano is very good, but Machado is, well, Machado.

Regardless, this has been a commendable offseason for the Mets front office. Keon Broxton could certainly contribute some inkling of speed New York has missed for years, and there's versatility now because of Lowrie and the questionable JD Davis trade that allows depth that we haven't seen in a while. But just from a fan's perspective BVW said, "We will win now, we will win in the future…" Shockingly, I do believe a 7-10 year deal to Machado or Harper helps accomplish this.

How does this team approach winning differently from other teams, and how does it shape its identity?

JARRETT: They really value familiarity and guys that they know. You see that most obviously in the Jeurys Familia signing. He's a well-liked former Met (setting aside for a moment whether he should be), and frankly they paid a bit of a premium to bring him back as a familiar face to the clubhouse. It's rare to see a player in his prime moved at the deadline and then brought back the next offseason, and yet they've done it in consecutive offseasons now with Familia and Jay Bruce. This also manifests in less obvious ways; Jed Lowrie isn't a former Met, but he's a guy with a lot of connections to current Mets staff, and a guy they've been rumored to be after for awhile now.

They also tend to aim at the high-80s or low-90s for a win total and look to surf in on positive variance and deadline acquisitions. When this works like it did in 2015, it *works*, but the goal here seems to be more perpetual contention than perpetual dominance. I do appreciate, purely as a fan, that they're trying to compete right now, even if they could try harder. Many teams with the same level of existing talent base and restrictions have went the other way.

KATE: I mean, if you want to talk about guys they've been lusting after forever, Cano is right there.

But I do agree with you that the Mets want to win. They may not be going about it the way I would like them to, but they're trying to in their own convoluted way. The middling years in the early 2010s really sucked, but I think at this point, we know that tanking doesn't work on its own, so yeah, I'll watch an 87-win team over an 82-win team, even if neither makes the playoffs.

Predictions?
KATE: 88-74, second place.
TYLER: 84-78, third place.
JARRETT: 87-75, second place, and the second Wild Card.

Performance Graphs

2018 Hit List Ranking

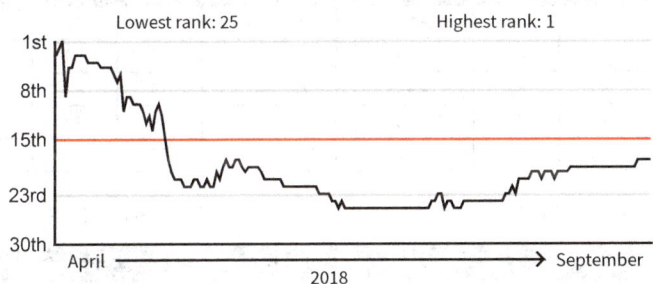

Committed Payroll (in millions)

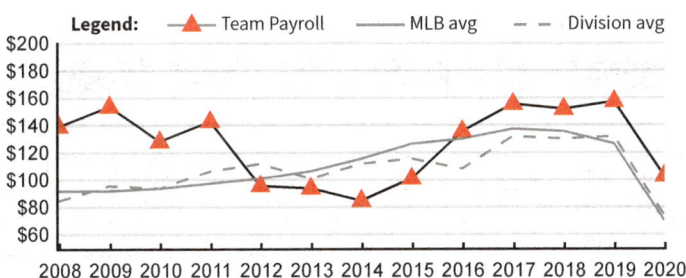

Farm System Ranking

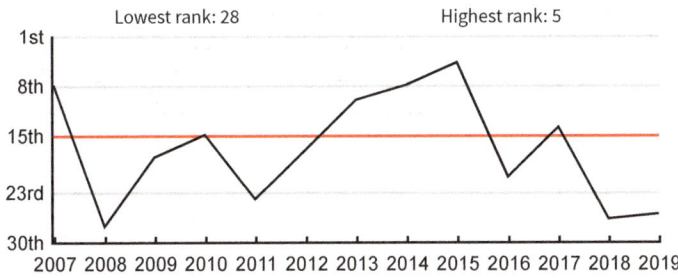

2018 Team Performance

ACTUAL STANDINGS

Team	W	L	Pct
ATL	90	72	.555
WAS	82	80	.506
PHI	80	82	.493
NYN	**77**	**85**	**.475**
MIA	63	98	.391

THIRD-ORDER STANDINGS

Team	W	L	Pct
ATL	94	68	.580
WAS	91	71	.561
NYN	**79**	**83**	**.487**
PHI	79	83	.487
MIA	63	98	.391

TOP HITTERS

Player	WARP
Brandon Nimmo	3.6
Todd Frazier	2.5
Michael Conforto	1.8

TOP PITCHERS

Player	WARP
Jacob deGrom	8
Noah Syndergaard	5
Zack Wheeler	4.8

VITAL STATISTICS

Statistic Name	Value	Rank
Pythagenpat	.479	17th
Runs Scored per Game	4.17	23rd
Runs Allowed per Game	4.36	16th
Deserved Runs Created Plus	91	22nd
Deserved Run Average	3.82	5th
Fielding Independent Pitching	3.93	9th
Defensive Efficiency Rating	.705	17th
Batter Age	28.4	20th
Pitcher Age	27.9	14th
Salary	$150.6M	12th
Marginal $ per Marginal Win	$4.8M	10th
Disabled List Days	$1,753.0M	30th
$ on DL	45%	30th

2019 Team Projections

PROJECTED STANDINGS

Team	W	L	Pct	+/-
WAS	89	73	.549	+7
NYN	**87**	**75**	**.537**	**+10**
ATL	85	77	.524	-5
PHI	85	77	.524	+5
MIA	68	94	.419	+5

TOP PROJECTED HITTERS

Player	WARP
Jeff McNeil	2.8
Robinson Cano	2.8
Brandon Nimmo	2.7

TOP PROJECTED PITCHERS

Player	WARP
Jacob deGrom	4.1
Noah Syndergaard	3.3
Steven Matz	1.8

FARM SYSTEM REPORT

Top Prospect	Number of Top 101 Prospects
Andres Gimenez, #38	2

KEY DEDUCTIONS

Player	WARP
Wilmer Flores	2.1
Jay Bruce	1.4
Kevin Plawecki	0.7
Anthony Swarzak	0.3

KEY ADDITIONS

Player	WARP
Robinson Cano	2.8
Wilson Ramos	1.8
Edwin Diaz	1.6
J.D. Davis	1.4
Carlos Gomez	1.3
Jed Lowrie	1.3
Adeiny Hechavarria	0.9
David Peterson	0.6
Justin Wilson	0.3

Team Personnel

General Manager
Brodie Van Wagenen

VP, Assistant General Manager, Scouting and Player Development
Allard Baird

Assistant General Manager
Adam Guttridge

SVP, Assistant General Manager
John Ricco

VP, International and Amateur Scouting
Tommy Tanous

Manager
Mickey Callaway

BP Alumni
Russell A. Carleton

Citi Field Stats

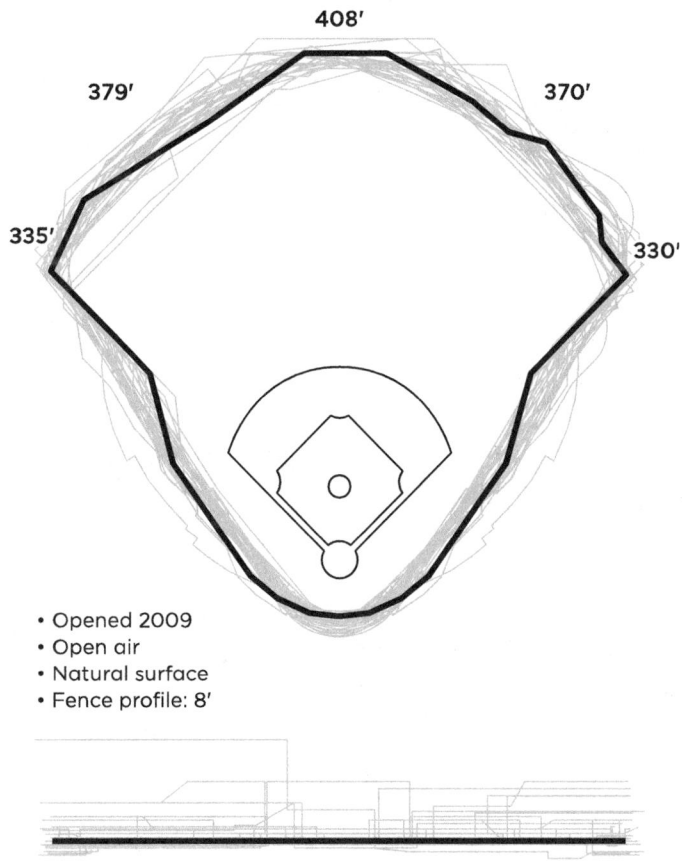

- Opened 2009
- Open air
- Natural surface
- Fence profile: 8'

Three-Year Park Factors

Runs	Runs/RH	Runs/LH	HR/RH	HR/LH
94	94	94	100	95

Mets Team Analysis

Are the Mets funny?

Their stadium literally caught fire. They lost a game 25-4 (it was 25-1 after eight innings). They lost another game 15-0 (it was 1-0 after seven innings). They hit out of order. They canceled a replica batting practice pullover giveaway hours before it was scheduled because of a "quality control issue". Their offense at one point cobbled together the lowest batting average by any major-league team in a homestand of at least seven games since 1900. One of their star pitchers missed time due to hand-foot-and-mouth disease, an illness most common with young children (he is 26 and does not have kids.) Their other star pitcher was the near unanimous National League Cy Young winner, but he won with a 10-9 record because of historically low run support. He broke a record by winning the Cy Young with the fewest wins ever. By three.

This all happened in 2018.

So far, yeah, this is fairly funny. Nobody died in the physical sense, so even better.

There is more, unfortunately.

The Mets play in New York, the largest media market on planet Earth, and they haven't even gotten their Amazon headquarters yet. There have always been and always will be literally millions of Mets fans that are willing to go to their games, even the day after they lose 25-4. The team owns 65 percent of SNY, the network that exclusively broadcasts their games locally. Each owner in Major League Baseball before 2018, which by definition includes Fred Wilpon, the principal owner of this team, received a reported $50 million from the BAMTech sale. Fred, his son Jeff (the team COO), and team president Saul Katz went from possibly needing to pony up over $1 billion to the victims of Bernie Madoff's Ponzi scheme in 2011 to being ordered to pay up $61 million five years later, in installments. It was estimated that ownership made $46 million in local TV revenues in 2016 alone. The $525 million national television contract is split among all 30 teams. There was enough money for Jeff to spend $20 million on an eSports team.

The Mets have money, is what I'm getting at here.

Yet the team's Opening Day payroll in 2018 was about $150.5 million, down from the previous year. You would have needed to add more than $46 million to reach the luxury tax threshold. Even if you factor in the famous yearly installment they have to pay an old friend every July 1, they are more than $45 million away.

New York Mets 2019

The threshold is a soft salary cap. You could, technically, go over that number. The other professional baseball franchise in New York went over the luxury tax threshold every year since the tax's existence, up until 2018. That team almost always makes the postseason, unlike the Mets. Every owner in baseball now has become an industrial strength scoundrel and act as if the soft salary cap is a hard one, but the Wilpons are their heroes.

Ownership did not put their monies towards math. They had three full-time employees in their analytics department last season. The Yankees had 20. In a 2018 season post mortem, Jeff Wilpon claimed[1] the former general manager Sandy Alderson was cool with just the three. This was a particularly ridiculous and pathetic claim because he said this after Alderson resigned due to the return of his cancer, and Alderson was literally the mentor to Billy Beane, the man behind *Moneyball*. *The Athletic* reported that Jeff Wilpon's obvious lie was a lie within 24 hours of the statement.

Published reports claimed that the teeny tiny analytics department was not even listened to anyway. They were against[2] the Jay Bruce and Jason Vargas signings. Vargas finished with a 5.77 ERA. Bruce's WARP in 2018 was 0.12.

When Omar Minaya was GM of the Mets, according to a report that came out recently, he wanted one of his interns, a young man named David Stearns, promoted to a full-time analytics person. Fred and Jeff would not pony up the money[3]. David now runs the Milwaukee Brewers, who are really good without spending that much money.

It appears you are spitting out your beverage. This is funny to you. Good! I'll keep going.

Jeff also claimed Sandy Alderson's regime was responsible for the lack of big free agent spending. He then did not commit to signing a top tier free agent like Manny Machado. Jeff definitely did not bring up the fact that his father Fred more than once saved Terry Collins' job[4] when Sandy Alderson wanted to fire him, or that Fred rejected a trade Sandy had made with Cleveland for Jason Kipnis because of money[5], after refusing to tell Sandy Alderson how much money he could spend in the first place[6].

The Mets would have you know some other organizations do not spend to the limit and still succeed. Those organizations are able to identify their young talent and exploit those youths' talents before they reach free agency.

Yeah, the Mets do not do that. They have been blessed with good and potentially great young talent, one assumes usually by accident, based on how well they can evaluate their own talent. We all know The Tale of Justin Turner, and the Daniel Murphy Saga, but much less know of the following: Brandon Nimmo blossomed into an above-average everyday player in 2018, even though he was supposed to be blocked by Jay Bruce. It was revealed during this past season that when Wallace Matthews of Forbes asked the then-manager of the Mets, Terry Collins, why Nimmo wasn't playing regularly during the second half of the 2017 season when the Mets were comfortably out of playoff contention, Collins said, "Oh, we know what we got", and not in a fun, good vibes way. When Terry Collins was "reassigned" after the 2017 season, he became a special assistant to the General Manager. He was seen at various points during 2018 overlooking minor league games, growing increasingly certain of what they got.

The Mets featured Jose Reyes, a wayyyyyyy-past-his-prime former star player who had been suspended for 51 games for alleged domestic violence. Mickey Callaway started him eight games in a nine day stretch last July, instead of letting rookies show their potential worth. At least, that is what some of this team's fan base believed, because they mistakenly believed the manager was in charge of such decisions. Fred Wilpon loves the way-past-his-prime player, and more specifically loved how inexpensive he was for the team. And he loved these things while reportedly sitting in the manager's office before and after games after he said he would not do that anymore.

Reyes was so bad, and the usage of this player so egregious, that the critically acclaimed in-game announcers—Gary Cohen, Ron Darling, and Keith Hernandez—who it should again be noted work for a network 65 percent owned by Fred Wilpon—repeatedly noted with exasperation that Jose Reyes was starting, never once blaming the manager, but stopping short of saying who they all knew was really responsible. The final indignity was when everybody with a functioning brain asked the Mets why their sizzling hot second base prospect in Triple-A, Jeff McNeil, was in Triple-A, and were told with a straight face it was because the second base prospect could not possibly play other positions like, say, third base, where it just so happened Jose Reyes was currently playing. McNeil began to play third base in Triple-A almost immediately, and played there sometimes after he was eventually promoted, too. McNeil finished his rookie year 120th out of 1,270 players in bWARP. Reyes finished tied for 1,215th place.

Reyes was so unbelievably awful that he will surely not be signed yet again for 2019, but you never know. What we do know as of this writing is the Mets did bring back Jeurys Familia, when other relief pitchers who have never been suspended for a domestic incident were available, including Andrew Miller, a great pitcher who had his best seasons with Mickey Callaway as his pitching coach. Did I mention the first majority owner of the Mets was Joan Whitney Payson, the first female owner of a professional baseball franchise who did not inherit it?

You are shaking your head and looking disgusted. Fair enough.

Might as well bring up Brodie Van Wagenen. The Mets hired the prominent agent as their new general manager. This raised red flags around the game, since he might possess inside information with some former clients, some of whom are still on the team. Cynical thinking, sure. Maybe they just hired him because his father-in-law was Neil Armstrong, and that's cool. But then Noah Syndergaard, a client of Van Wagenen's old agency, was suddenly very much on the trading block.

Not that it matters. Peter Gammons said as far back as 10 years ago that Jeff Wilpon is the real general manager of the Mets[7]. Jeff has recently confirmed he has final say on all personnel matters[8].

Okay, I see you shaking your head and trying to moonwalk away from me. But you are also smirking. This is still kind of funny to you! Just definitely no longer ha ha funny.

Yes, I know I sound cynical. There's a new sheriff in town! And the gun the mayor gives his sheriffs is a gun made of newspaper from 1955.

Fine, Robinson Cano is still good. Edwin Diaz is exciting. Weird the Mets had to trade top prospects and did not spend money on players who won't be 40 years old when their contract expires but hey, Wilson Ramos is good when healthy.

Ah, "when healthy." I hate that phrase so.

David Wright, the one who discovered he suffered from spinal stenosis at the age of 32, played one final game in 2018 and had himself an emotional farewell. My television screen definitely got a little blurry that evening. He could not use the word "retire" though, out of ownership's fear insurance would stop paying 75 percent of his salary. While collecting those insurance funds (but not applying them back to the payroll budget), Jeff used one of the franchise's most beloved players ever as an excuse for their lack of spending. That was fun.

Yoenis Cespedes played hurt for a month and everybody with eyes knew it. He returned two months later to play one game, then announced after that game he needed surgery on both of his heels. He did not play another game in 2018, and is due out for at least half of 2019.

Oh goodness, I almost forgot Matt Harvey. After he was demoted to the bullpen he told the *New York Times* beat writer "I don't [expletive] want to" talk to the media about it. He was traded, and most fans were shocked he did not immediately become an ace again, because they've internalized this belief they are "snakebitten," as Fred Wilpon once confirmed to The New Yorker years ago.

A multi-millionaire wants the fans to believe this franchise's *raison d'être* is truly what it appeared to be since its 1962 inception as presented by Jimmy Breslin: a representation of New Yorkers of the lower and middle classes who could not relate to those Yankees who were compared to U.S. Steel and Coca-Cola. This Goofus and Gallant dynamic is ingrained, destined to play out in men hitting horsehide with wooden sticks until the end of civilized times, except we now do not bother mentioning the middle class because that disappeared, and we switch out the sugar water conglomerate with Amazon and keep telling that story. Got it? Or maybe we factor in this team's ownership's constant hoodwinking and overall shadiness? Do we factor in both? Does it even matter?

Does any of this matter?

Because the Mets might be pretty good, despite all of *motions to the universe* this. They made the World Series not all that long ago! Their farm system is no longer considered one of the worst in the sport. This team, every damn spring, by virtue of always plotting and scheming their way to a projected .500 season but with a glossy sheen of Pretty Decent *When Healthy*, is always on the cusp of Something Painfully Bad or Something Special. Usually, it's the former. Every so often, it proves to be the latter. It happens often enough to always keep you interested. God, it is always entertaining. They always get you in the end.

And now you are pointing and laughing at me. With me? It doesn't matter.

—*Roger Cormier is an author of Baseball Prospectus.*

1. Anderson, R.J. "Mets ownership blamed Sandy Alderson for lack of spending and analytics staff." CBSSports.com. Accessed 26 December 2018. https://www.cbssports.com/mlb/news/mets-ownership-blamed-sandy-alderson-for-lack-of-spending-and-analytics-staff/

2. Ehalt, Matt. "NY Mets may be limiting GM field if they're not open to fully embracing analytics." Northjersey.com. Accessed 26 December 2018. https://www.northjersey.com/story/sports/mlb/mets/2018/10/04/ny-mets-may-limiting-gm-field-not-open-fully-embracing-analytics/1522928002/

3. Healey, Tim. "Mets experts at picking future executives but not keeping them." Newsday. Accessed 26 December 2018. https://www.newsday.com/sports/baseball/mets/mets-have-watched-homegrown-gm-candidates-blossom-elsewhere-1.21909689

4. Carig, Marc. "Sources: Mets owner Fred Wilpon protected Terry Collins from getting fired." Newsday. Accessed 26 December 2018. https://www.newsday.com/sports/baseball/mets/sources-mets-owner-fred-wilpon-protected-terry-collins-from-getting-fired-1.14297441

5. Carig, Marc. "Without another strong arm in the rotation, the Mets are doomed to mediocrity." The Athletic. Accessed 26 December 2018. https://theathletic.com/238391/2018/02/12/carig-without-another-strong-arm-in-the-rotation-the-mets-are-doomed-to-mediocrity/, January 5, 1952, p. 10.

6. Carig, Marc. "Mets analysis: Wilpons need to be more transparent about payroll, offseason moves." Newsday. Accessed 26 December 2018. https://www.newsday.com/sports/baseball/mets/mets-jeff-wilpon-1.15485312, January 5, 1952, p. 10.

7. Cerrone, Matthew. "Gammons: Jeff Wilpon is GM of the Mets." SNY Mets Blog. Accessed 26 December 2018. https://www.sny.tv/mets/news/gammons-jeff-wilpon-is-gm-of-the-mets/149375936

8. Ehalt, Matt. "Jeff Wilpon admits frustration with how the Mets have performed." Northjersey.com. Accessed 26 December 2018. https://www.northjersey.com/story/sports/mlb/mets/2018/06/26/ny-mets-coo-jeff-wilpon-says-mets-have-not-met-their-expectations/736653002/

Part 2: Player Analysis

Robinson Cano 2B

Born: 10/22/82 Age: 36 Bats: L Throws: R
Height: 6'0" Weight: 210 Origin: International Free Agent, 2001

YEAR	TEAM	LVL	AGE	PA	R	2B	3B	HR	RBI	BB	K	SB	CS	AVG/OBP/SLG
2016	SEA	MLB	33	715	107	33	2	39	103	47	100	0	1	.298/.350/.533
2017	SEA	MLB	34	648	79	33	0	23	97	49	85	1	0	.280/.338/.453
2018	SEA	MLB	35	348	44	22	0	10	50	32	47	0	0	.303/.374/.471
2019	NYN	MLB	36	594	67	30	2	18	74	50	89	1	1	.276/.343/.440

Breakout: 1% Improve: 20% Collapse: 22% Attrition: 5% MLB: 90%
Comparables: Chase Utley, Del Pratt, Carlos Guillen

With a contract like Cano's, everything gets measured in the millions. How many millions left on the ledger? How many millions earned over the entire career? How many millions did the Mariners save over his 80-game suspension for the banned substance Furosemide? How many millions earned per win produced on the field? Perhaps that's one of the biggest dangers of the mega-contract, because to focus so intently on the financial aspect is to obscure what is rapidly becoming one of the greatest careers any second baseman has ever had. Despite playing only half a season in 2018, Cano was, once again, one of the most productive players at the keystone position. At 36 there's plenty of reason to speculate how long he can do it, but until he actually shows noticeable degradation of skills the Mets should not feel any pressing need to move him anywhere else. His career is already one of the greats, one whose direct path to Cooperstown is hopefully not marred by a lapse in judgment or misreading of a pharmaceutical bottle. If he can maintain healthy, near-peak production for a few more seasons, he will have cemented himself as one of the four or five greatest second basemen of the modern era. Of the millions who have played baseball, that's not bad company.

YEAR	TEAM	LVL	AGE	PA	DRC+	VORP	BABIP	BRR	FRAA	WARP
2016	SEA	MLB	33	715	133	46.0	.299	-1.7	2B(157): 4.2	5.2
2017	SEA	MLB	34	648	108	23.1	.294	-2.0	2B(150): -7.3	1.7
2018	SEA	MLB	35	348	125	23.6	.329	-0.4	2B(69): -2.5, 1B(14): 0.3	1.8
2019	NYN	MLB	36	594	116	30.5	.300	-1.4	2B -2, 1B 0	2.8

Robinson Cano, *continued*

Batted Ball Distribution

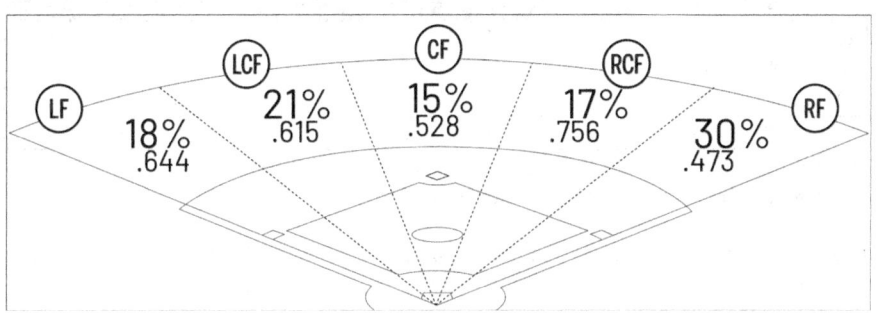

Strike Zone vs LHP   Strike Zone vs RHP

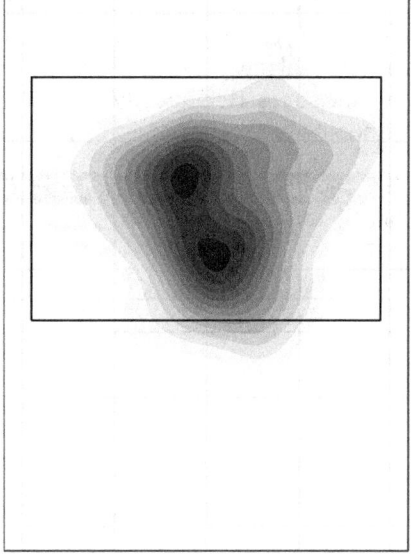

Yoenis Cespedes LF

Born: 10/18/85   Age: 33   Bats: R   Throws: R
Height: 5'10"   Weight: 220   Origin: International Free Agent, 2012

YEAR	TEAM	LVL	AGE	PA	R	2B	3B	HR	RBI	BB	K	SB	CS	AVG/OBP/SLG
2016	NYN	MLB	30	543	72	25	1	31	86	51	108	3	1	.280/.354/.530
2017	NYN	MLB	31	321	46	17	2	17	42	26	61	0	1	.292/.352/.540
2018	NYN	MLB	32	157	20	6	0	9	29	13	50	3	0	.262/.325/.496
2019	NYN	MLB	33	128	16	6	0	5	17	11	28	1	0	.261/.328/.443

Breakout: 0%   Improve: 25%   Collapse: 26%   Attrition: 6%   MLB: 97%
Comparables: Ryan Braun, Alfonso Soriano, Scott Hairston

For years, the Mets have played their brightest offensive star through a litany of injuries, both major and minor, in an attempt to get his potent bat into a sagging lineup. In 2018, the bill came due. Even as a hip flexor strain sucked months from his season, Cespedes was every bit the offensive dynamo advertised when the team acquired him. However, July brought with it the end of Cespedes' season. It will now be two heel surgeries and perhaps as much as a full year of rehab before he's likely to don a Mets uniform again. If he's back in the second half of 2019, expect him to be every bit the slugger he's always been: phenomenal raw power packed into a body that can barely contain it, bursting from the stress. He's already proven he can play through the pain, but the Mets are hoping there's less of it this year.

YEAR	TEAM	LVL	AGE	PA	DRC+	VORP	BABIP	BRR	FRAA	WARP
2016	NYN	MLB	30	543	132	48.4	.298	-1.9	LF(80): 7.7, CF(63): -5.2	3.8
2017	NYN	MLB	31	321	123	23.9	.316	-1.1	LF(74): 2.9	1.9
2018	NYN	MLB	32	157	99	11.1	.333	0.5	LF(35): 1.8	0.6
2019	NYN	MLB	33	128	124	7.6	.303	-0.1	LF 1	0.9

Yoenis Cespedes, continued

Batted Ball Distribution

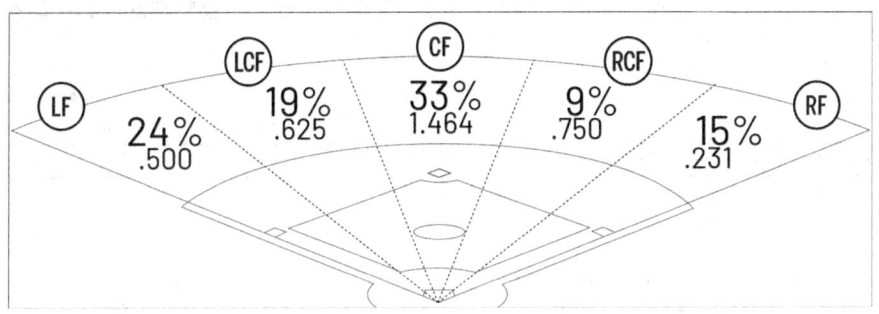

Strike Zone vs LHP   **Strike Zone vs RHP**

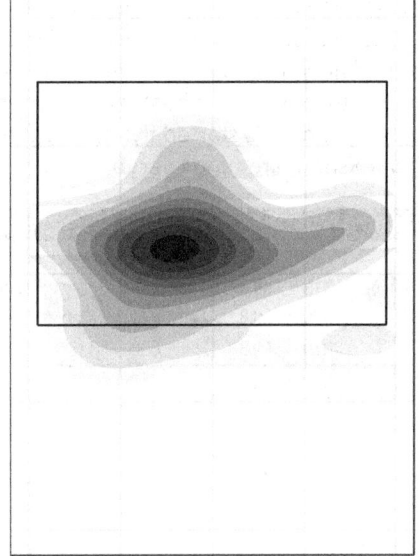

Michael Conforto OF

Born: 03/01/93 Age: 26 Bats: L Throws: R
Height: 6'1" Weight: 215 Origin: Round 1, 2014 Draft (#10 overall)

YEAR	TEAM	LVL	AGE	PA	R	2B	3B	HR	RBI	BB	K	SB	CS	AVG/OBP/SLG
2016	LVG	AAA	23	144	30	8	2	9	28	13	18	2	2	.422/.483/.727
2016	NYN	MLB	23	348	38	21	1	12	42	36	89	2	1	.220/.310/.414
2017	NYN	MLB	24	440	72	20	1	27	68	57	113	2	0	.279/.384/.555
2018	NYN	MLB	25	638	78	25	1	28	82	84	159	3	4	.243/.350/.448
2019	NYN	MLB	26	563	72	25	2	24	78	62	138	3	2	.255/.346/.461

Breakout: 3%   Improve: 59%   Collapse: 6%   Attrition: 5%   MLB: 99%
Comparables: Carlos Quentin, Carlos Gonzalez, Derek Dietrich

A miserable shoulder injury ended Conforto's All-Star 2017 season and threatened the start of his 2018 season as well. For well-trained Mets fans, it was quite a surprise how quickly he "recovered" and that he ended up seeing 153 games of duty last year, but the shoulder injury clearly affected his season throughout. He certainly did not appear healthy early in the year, and it showed in his offensive performance. Conforto couldn't regularly make his signature brand of loud contact, and he tried to adapt by being overly patient at the plate to find his way on base. By the second half of the season, his shoulder and stat line both looked a lot healthier. Scooter got more aggressive, the contact got louder, and balls started flying over the wall more regularly. A full season of total health should remind everyone just how rock-solid Conforto's offense can be.

YEAR	TEAM	LVL	AGE	PA	DRC+	VORP	BABIP	BRR	FRAA	WARP
2016	LVG	AAA	23	144	209	20.1	.446	-1.1	LF(18): 0.4, CF(6): -1.3	1.6
2016	NYN	MLB	23	348	90	12.6	.267	1.2	LF(73): 0.8, RF(9): 0.7	0.7
2017	NYN	MLB	24	440	133	47.8	.328	1.4	LF(52): 3.9, CF(43): -3.6	3.3
2018	NYN	MLB	25	638	112	36.2	.289	-4.2	LF(84): 1.1, CF(58): -7.3	1.8
2019	NYN	MLB	26	563	120	29.7	.302	-1.1	RF -2	2.6

Michael Conforto, continued

Batted Ball Distribution

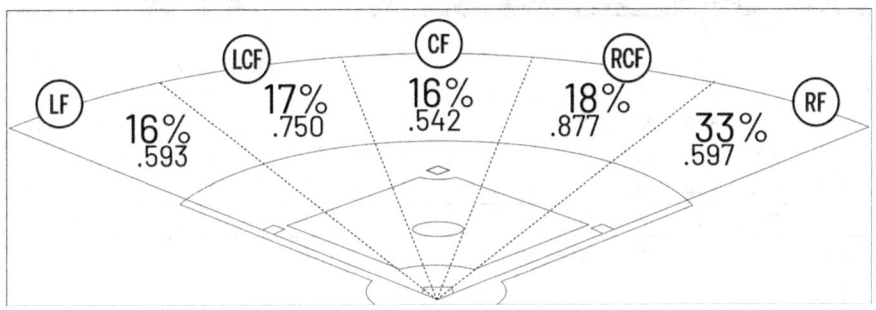

Strike Zone vs LHP

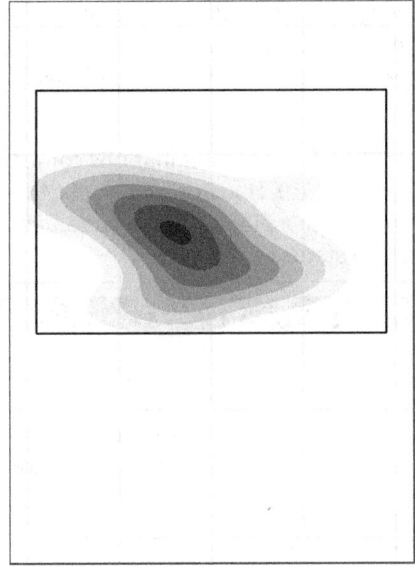

Strike Zone vs RHP

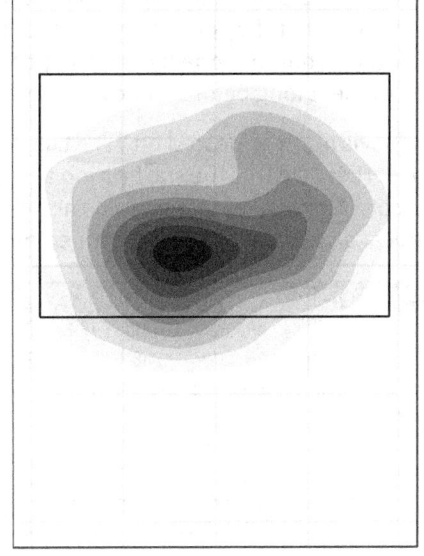

J.D. Davis 3B

Born: 04/27/93 Age: 26 Bats: R Throws: R
Height: 6'3" Weight: 225 Origin: Round 3, 2014 Draft (#75 overall)

YEAR	TEAM	LVL	AGE	PA	R	2B	3B	HR	RBI	BB	K	SB	CS	AVG/OBP/SLG
2016	CCH	AA	23	539	61	34	1	23	81	45	143	1	3	.268/.334/.485
2017	CCH	AA	24	388	49	18	0	21	60	31	90	5	2	.279/.340/.510
2017	FRE	AAA	24	73	10	5	0	5	18	9	18	0	0	.295/.370/.623
2017	HOU	MLB	24	68	8	4	0	4	7	4	20	1	1	.226/.279/.484
2018	FRE	AAA	25	377	56	25	2	17	81	36	69	3	0	.342/.406/.583
2018	HOU	MLB	25	113	9	2	0	1	5	10	29	0	0	.175/.248/.223
2019	NYN	MLB	26	299	37	14	1	11	38	25	69	1	0	.259/.324/.441

Breakout: 6%   Improve: 36%   Collapse: 10%   Attrition: 27%   MLB: 70%
Comparables: Todd Frazier, Richie Shaffer, David Freese

The later years of "The Late Show with David Letterman" featured a bit called "Is This Anything?" in which the host would introduce the segment, the main curtain would rise, some oddball performer would do her or his shtick, the curtain would fall, and Dave and Paul would spend about 15 seconds debating whether what they just saw was anything or not. It was a perfect piece of irreverent humor done by the very people who were on the vanguard of that movement long before it became popular.

Davis never appeared on "The Late Show," but if roster machinations come to bear that he earns the starting job at first base in 2019, Houston will be playing a bit of a high-stakes game of "Is This Anything?" with a player that so far (albeit still at a young age) seems destined for Quad-A status.

YEAR	TEAM	LVL	AGE	PA	DRC+	VORP	BABIP	BRR	FRAA	WARP
2016	CCH	AA	23	539	128	34.0	.331	-2.6	3B(101): -6.1, LF(4): 0.3	1.2
2017	CCH	AA	24	388	132	30.0	.317	-0.5	3B(73): 6.1, 1B(3): -0.2	2.2
2017	FRE	AAA	24	73	140	7.9	.317	-0.4	3B(13): 2.1, 1B(4): 0.0	0.7
2017	HOU	MLB	24	68	78	1.7	.256	-0.2	3B(22): 0.5, P(2): 0.0	0.1
2018	FRE	AAA	25	377	163	39.4	.385	0.0	3B(51): 4.2, LF(11): -0.8	3.6
2018	HOU	MLB	25	113	68	-7.3	.233	-0.5	3B(23): 0.9, 1B(13): 0.0	0.0
2019	NYN	MLB	26	299	121	15.8	.306	-0.4	LF -1, 1B 0	1.4

J.D. Davis, continued

Batted Ball Distribution

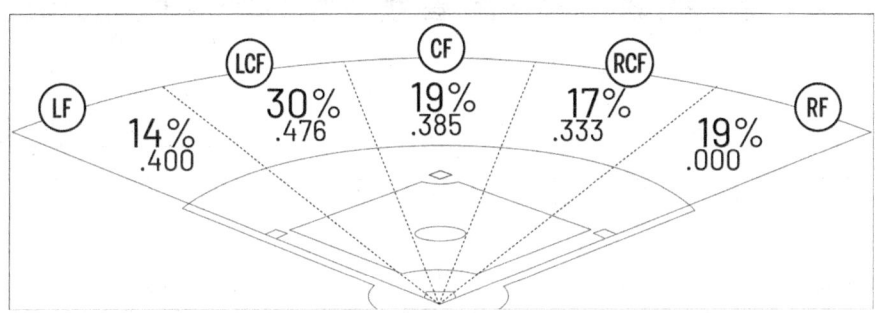

Strike Zone vs LHP   **Strike Zone vs RHP**

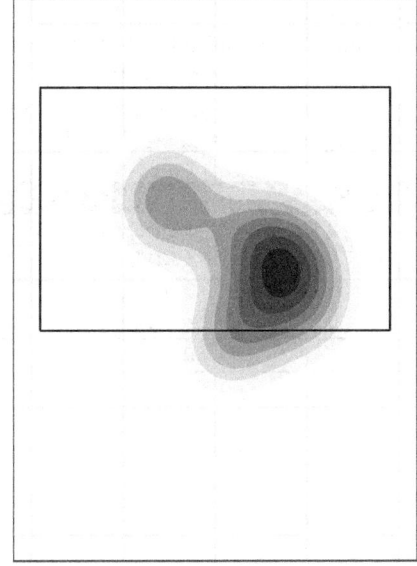
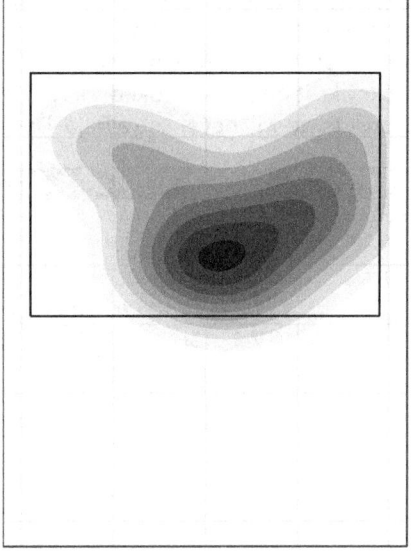

Rajai Davis LF

Born: 10/19/80   Age: 38   Bats: R   Throws: R
Height: 5'10"   Weight: 195   Origin: Round 38, 2001 Draft (#1134 overall)

YEAR	TEAM	LVL	AGE	PA	R	2B	3B	HR	RBI	BB	K	SB	CS	AVG/OBP/SLG
2016	CLE	MLB	35	495	74	23	2	12	48	33	106	43	6	.249/.306/.388
2017	OAK	MLB	36	328	49	17	2	5	18	26	70	26	6	.233/.294/.353
2017	BOS	MLB	36	38	7	2	0	0	2	1	13	3	1	.250/.289/.306
2018	CLE	MLB	37	216	33	6	1	1	6	11	48	21	7	.224/.278/.281
2019	NYN	MLB	38	251	35	11	1	4	19	18	56	20	5	.236/.298/.349

Breakout: 1%   Improve: 17%   Collapse: 15%   Attrition: 27%   MLB: 72%
Comparables: Al Nixon, Devon White, Mike Kreevich

If you've tuned in to a national baseball broadcast in the last, oh, 15 years or so, you may have heard a former player lamenting the death of small ball and the vanishing of stolen bases. If Mr. Davis ever retires and becomes an announcer, he would certainly have more right to make the complaint than former first basemen or pitchers. Despite his advanced age, Davis still swiped more than 20 bags in part-time duty, as Cleveland brought back their World Series hero in a desperate attempt to throw anyone and anything at their outfield situation. He never possessed any real power or patience and his ability to hit for average looks like it might be cooked. His glove may not be too far behind. Even so, one suspects we will never see a Rajai Davis in the majors who can't steal a base.

YEAR	TEAM	LVL	AGE	PA	DRC+	VORP	BABIP	BRR	FRAA	WARP
2016	CLE	MLB	35	495	88	6.3	.299	3.7	CF(80): 3.5, LF(66): 1.4	1.7
2017	OAK	MLB	36	328	71	-1.5	.288	2.4	CF(79): -3.4, LF(19): -1.7	-0.4
2017	BOS	MLB	36	38	69	-1.0	.391	0.1	LF(6): -0.5, CF(4): -0.3	-0.1
2018	CLE	MLB	37	216	69	-4.4	.291	0.1	CF(47): 0.7, LF(30): -2.1	-0.3
2019	NYN	MLB	38	251	74	1.2	.293	0.6	CF 0, LF 0	0.1

Rajai Davis, continued

Batted Ball Distribution

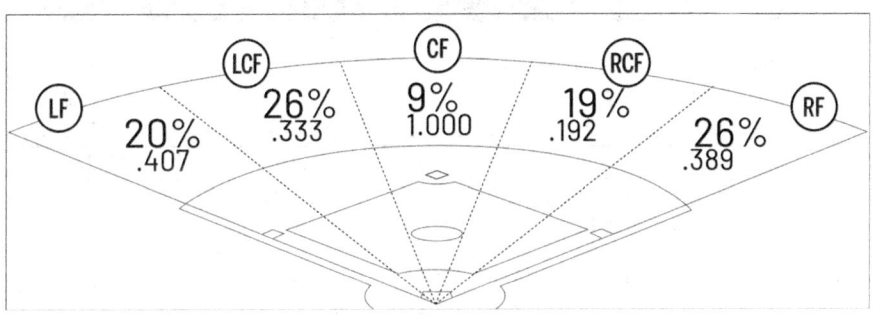

Strike Zone vs LHP   Strike Zone vs RHP

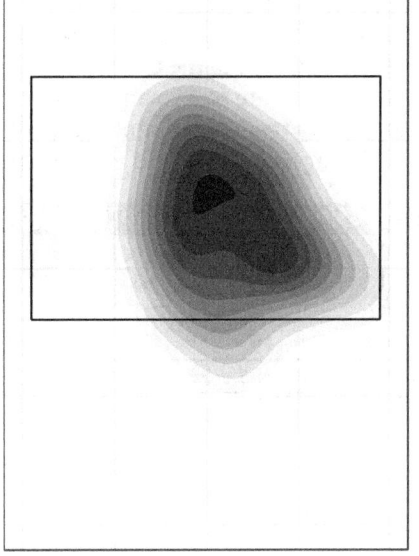

Todd Frazier 3B

Born: 02/12/86 Age: 33 Bats: R Throws: R
Height: 6'3" Weight: 220 Origin: Round 1, 2007 Draft (#34 overall)

YEAR	TEAM	LVL	AGE	PA	R	2B	3B	HR	RBI	BB	K	SB	CS	AVG/OBP/SLG
2016	CHA	MLB	30	666	89	21	0	40	98	64	163	15	5	.225/.302/.464
2017	CHA	MLB	31	335	41	15	0	16	44	48	71	4	3	.207/.328/.432
2017	NYA	MLB	31	241	33	4	1	11	32	35	54	0	0	.222/.365/.423
2018	NYN	MLB	32	472	54	18	0	18	59	48	112	9	4	.213/.303/.390
2019	NYN	MLB	33	303	37	11	1	11	37	32	70	5	2	.223/.317/.398

Breakout: 1% Improve: 28% Collapse: 11% Attrition: 5% MLB: 94%
Comparables: David Freese, Scott Rolen, Carlos Guillen

The greatest trick the devil ever pulled was convincing the world he didn't exist. He's got nothing on Frazier, who fell into the stands to catch an Alex Verdugo pop fly, dropped the baseball, but swapped a nearby rubber toy ball to convince the umpires that he had pulled off an incredible diving grab. A second, less impressive trick has been the way Frazier has carried a reputation as a powerful slugger into the later stages of his career, when really he's getting by on his defense and near-average batting lines. Known for his durability, Frazier made the first two trips to the DL of his career in 2018 and flashed solid numbers both at the start of the season and after his second stint in August, but faded as those stretches of the season went on. He's a serviceable second-division starter and a convincing sleight-of-hand artist, but not the offensive threat he once was.

YEAR	TEAM	LVL	AGE	PA	DRC+	VORP	BABIP	BRR	FRAA	WARP
2016	CHA	MLB	30	666	113	27.2	.236	2.4	3B(149): -2.4, 1B(7): -1.1	3.2
2017	CHA	MLB	31	335	113	12.0	.214	-0.4	3B(67): 2.2, 1B(4): 0.5	1.9
2017	NYA	MLB	31	241	113	10.2	.244	0.2	3B(66): 1.0	1.4
2018	NYN	MLB	32	472	99	24.0	.241	2.5	3B(109): 5.9	2.5
2019	NYN	MLB	33	303	101	8.8	.262	-0.2	3B 0, 1B 0	0.8

Todd Frazier, continued

Batted Ball Distribution

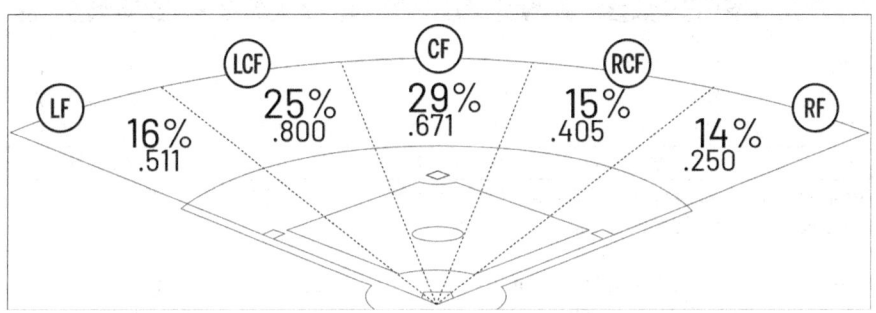

Strike Zone vs LHP **Strike Zone vs RHP**

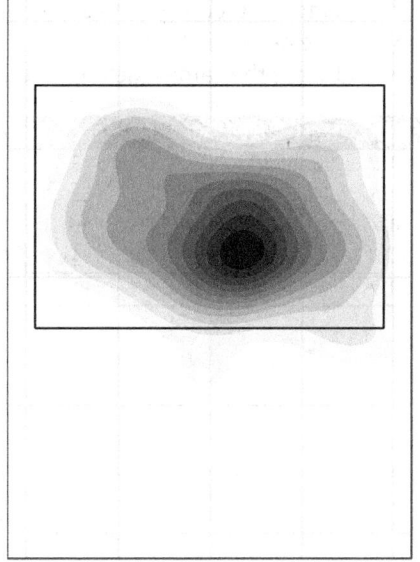

Carlos Gomez RF

Born: 12/04/85 Age: 33 Bats: R Throws: R
Height: 6'3" Weight: 220 Origin: International Free Agent, 2002

YEAR	TEAM	LVL	AGE	PA	R	2B	3B	HR	RBI	BB	K	SB	CS	AVG/OBP/SLG
2016	HOU	MLB	30	323	27	16	1	5	29	21	100	13	2	.210/.272/.322
2016	TEX	MLB	30	130	18	6	0	8	24	13	36	5	3	.284/.362/.543
2017	TEX	MLB	31	426	51	23	1	17	51	31	127	13	5	.255/.340/.462
2018	TBA	MLB	32	408	42	15	2	9	32	25	103	12	3	.208/.298/.336
2019	NYN	MLB	33	391	47	17	2	11	43	31	105	13	4	.227/.321/.376

Breakout: 2%   Improve: 23%   Collapse: 24%   Attrition: 16%   MLB: 88%
Comparables: Casey Blake, Hank Bauer, Laynce Nix

Gomez was a negative in terms of his 2018 offensive production, but his leadership in a clubhouse that lost its stability (Evan Longoria) prior to the season and its voice (Chris Archer) midway through will last beyond his .208 batting average. Coming off one of the worst seasons of his career, it is fair to wonder if we've seen the last of Gomez as a useful player. He'll likely get a few more chances either way. He's a decent defender still and has some remaining pop, but he never did learn to lay off bad pitches. Once Gomez does hang it up, it would serve the game if he remained involved in some capacity.

YEAR	TEAM	LVL	AGE	PA	DRC+	VORP	BABIP	BRR	FRAA	WARP
2016	HOU	MLB	30	323	83	-3.1	.300	3.9	CF(78): -4.0	0.4
2016	TEX	MLB	30	130	83	9.5	.347	0.4	LF(28): 1.2, CF(7): -0.1	0.2
2017	TEX	MLB	31	426	101	17.0	.336	-0.7	CF(102): -2.3	1.2
2018	TBA	MLB	32	408	84	-0.4	.266	3.6	RF(100): 5.4, CF(4): -0.1	1.0
2019	NYN	MLB	33	391	96	10.4	.302	1.4	RF 2, CF 0	1.3

Carlos Gomez, continued

Batted Ball Distribution

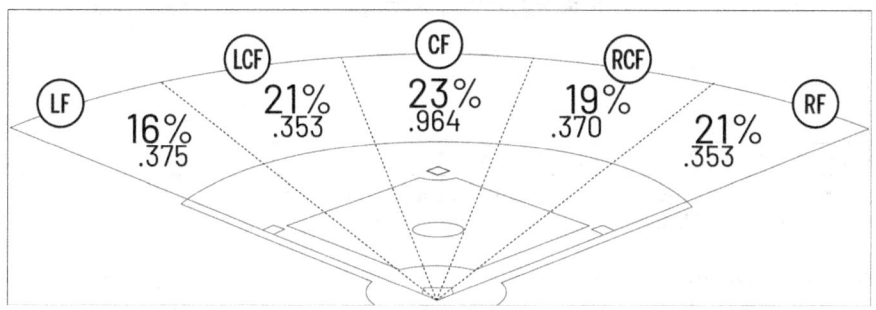

Strike Zone vs LHP

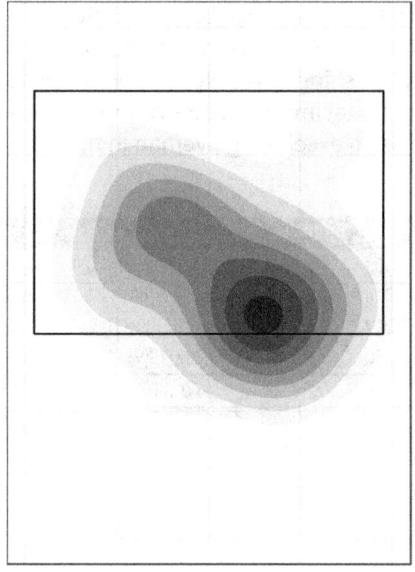

Strike Zone vs RHP

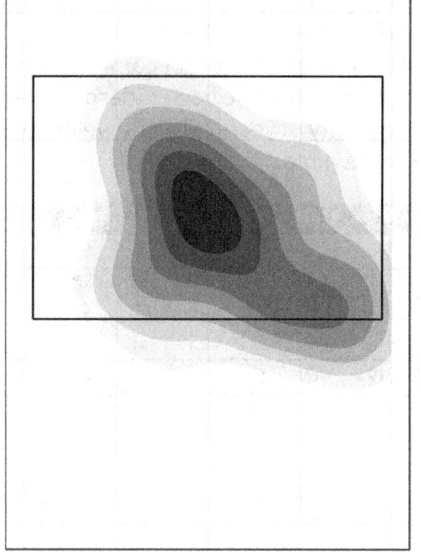

Luis Guillorme INF

Born: 09/27/94 Age: 24 Bats: L Throws: R
Height: 5'10" Weight: 195 Origin: Round 10, 2013 Draft (#296 overall)

YEAR	TEAM	LVL	AGE	PA	R	2B	3B	HR	RBI	BB	K	SB	CS	AVG/OBP/SLG
2016	SLU	A+	21	505	47	16	2	1	46	43	63	4	2	.263/.332/.315
2017	BIN	AA	22	558	70	20	0	1	43	72	55	4	3	.283/.376/.331
2018	NYN	MLB	23	74	4	2	0	0	5	7	3	1	0	.209/.284/.239
2018	LVG	AAA	23	281	41	15	2	3	33	30	39	2	1	.304/.380/.417
2019	NYN	MLB	24	140	14	6	1	3	14	11	24	0	0	.254/.317/.389

Breakout: 16%   Improve: 27%   Collapse: 0%   Attrition: 21%   MLB: 37%
Comparables: Dixon Machado, Jace Peterson, Christian Colon

Perhaps no player in the Mets' system was held down for as little reason as Guillorme, and that's saying something when Peter Alonso doesn't even get a September call-up. An exceptional defensive infielder, Guillorme has probably done all he needs to get a long look as a utility player ... except figure out how to stop the Mets from rostering Jose Reyes. While Reyes was racking up negative value (and PR), Guillorme shuttled back and forth between Vegas and New York—which normally sounds like fun but isn't the best way to develop an infielder—and never got comfortable in his Flushing looks. No, he's not likely to hit for much game power (despite the occasional impressive BP round), but he has plenty of years left to prove his worth as an excellent gloveman in the Adam Everett mold.

YEAR	TEAM	LVL	AGE	PA	DRC+	VORP	BABIP	BRR	FRAA	WARP
2016	SLU	A+	21	505	94	9.9	.303	0.1	SS(72): -1.6, 2B(52): 4.0	0.7
2017	BIN	AA	22	558	115	26.0	.316	3.4	2B(72): 4.1, SS(58): -2.1	2.4
2018	NYN	MLB	23	74	92	-0.5	.219	0.7	3B(14): -1.8, 2B(8): -0.5	0.0
2018	LVG	AAA	23	281	107	12.3	.350	0.3	SS(54): 1.9, 2B(9): -1.4	1.3
2019	NYN	MLB	24	140	85	2.4	.278	-0.2	SS 0, 3B -1	0.1

Luis Guillorme, continued

Batted Ball Distribution

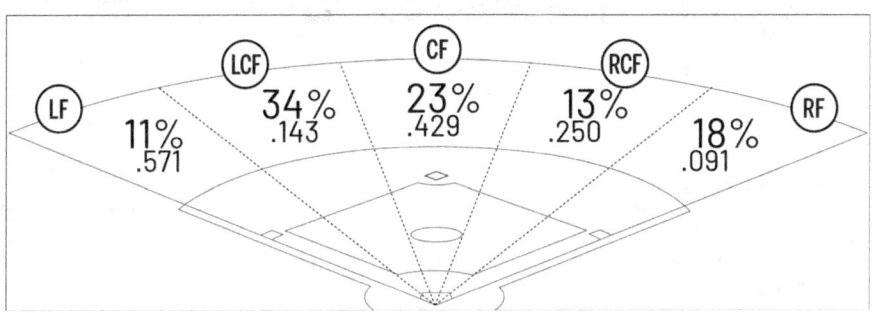

Strike Zone vs LHP   **Strike Zone vs RHP**

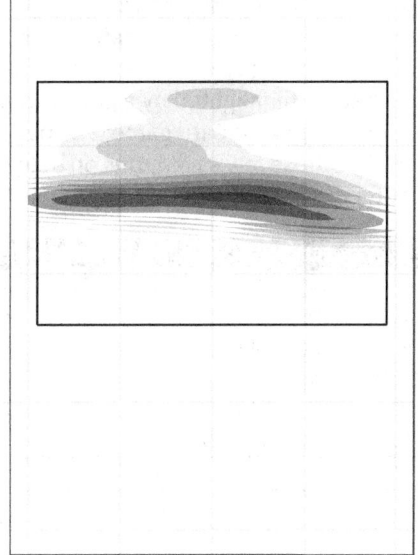

Adeiny Hechavarria SS

Born: 04/15/89 Age: 30 Bats: R Throws: R
Height: 6'0" Weight: 195 Origin: International Free Agent, 2010

YEAR	TEAM	LVL	AGE	PA	R	2B	3B	HR	RBI	BB	K	SB	CS	AVG/OBP/SLG
2016	MIA	MLB	27	547	52	17	6	3	38	33	73	1	0	.236/.283/.311
2017	MIA	MLB	28	67	8	2	1	1	6	1	9	0	0	.277/.288/.385
2017	TBA	MLB	28	281	29	12	4	7	24	12	58	4	1	.257/.289/.411
2018	TBA	MLB	29	237	29	7	0	3	26	12	37	1	0	.258/.289/.332
2018	PIT	MLB	29	47	2	4	0	1	3	3	11	0	0	.233/.277/.395
2018	NYA	MLB	29	37	3	0	0	2	2	1	10	1	0	.194/.216/.361
2019	NYN	MLB	30	315	32	14	2	6	32	22	52	2	1	.255/.311/.381

Breakout: 5%   Improve: 30%   Collapse: 16%   Attrition: 25%   MLB: 97%
Comparables: Alex Cintron, Jack Wilson, Alcides Escobar

When you're a potential playoff team with important games in September, defensive replacements become a near-necessity as the rosters expand. So it makes sense that the Yankees acquired Hechavarria at the waiver trade deadline for that very purpose. With Didi Gregorius dealing with injury and Miguel Andujar dealing with... his defense, Hechavarria was a more than capable backup, playing 18 games and four out of the five playoff games in just that short span, highlighted by a jaw-dropping leaping grab he made in the seventh inning of the Wild Card game. The bat never came around, and it likely never will, but those few saved runs on defense down the stretch could benefit a contending team in the future.

YEAR	TEAM	LVL	AGE	PA	DRC+	VORP	BABIP	BRR	FRAA	WARP
2016	MIA	MLB	27	547	75	8.5	.269	6.5	SS(153): 2.3	1.7
2017	MIA	MLB	28	67	83	0.6	.309	-0.9	SS(19): -1.1	0.0
2017	TBA	MLB	28	281	85	5.7	.302	-1.3	SS(77): 3.4	1.0
2018	TBA	MLB	29	237	89	6.7	.290	1.5	SS(61): -1.3	0.8
2018	PIT	MLB	29	47	88	-1.2	.281	-1.3	SS(15): -1.1	-0.1
2018	NYA	MLB	29	37	88	-0.2	.208	0.1	SS(16): -1.4, 3B(4): -0.3	-0.1
2019	NYN	MLB	30	315	88	8.5	.290	0.9	SS 0, 3B 0	0.9

Adeiny Hechavarria, continued

Batted Ball Distribution

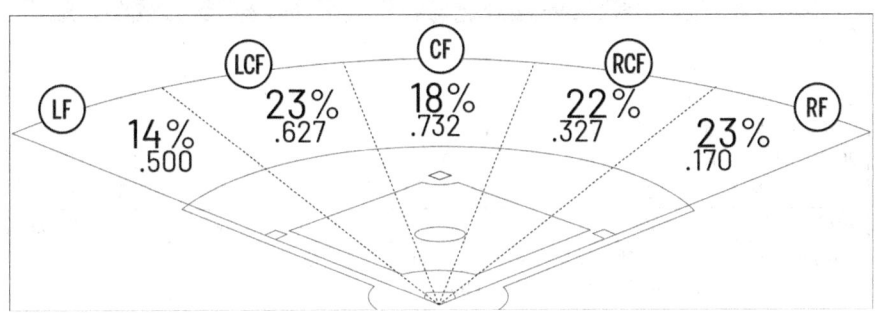

Strike Zone vs LHP **Strike Zone vs RHP**

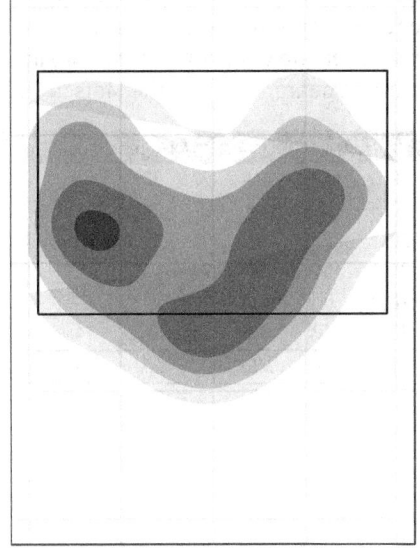

Dilson Herrera 2B

Born: 03/03/94 Age: 25 Bats: R Throws: R
Height: 5'10" Weight: 210 Origin: International Free Agent, 2010

YEAR	TEAM	LVL	AGE	PA	R	2B	3B	HR	RBI	BB	K	SB	CS	AVG/OBP/SLG
2016	LVG	AAA	22	389	61	24	2	13	55	27	72	6	7	.276/.327/.462
2016	LOU	AAA	22	80	10	0	2	2	9	11	15	1	2	.266/.372/.422
2017	LOU	AAA	23	265	31	9	1	7	42	15	61	2	4	.264/.312/.397
2018	DAY	A+	24	92	18	3	1	2	8	7	19	1	1	.298/.359/.429
2018	LOU	AAA	24	208	23	10	0	7	27	19	50	0	1	.297/.367/.465
2018	CIN	MLB	24	97	11	5	0	5	11	8	39	0	0	.184/.268/.414
2019	NYN	MLB	25	251	29	7	1	8	25	18	66	2	2	.219/.283/.356

Breakout: 12% Improve: 44% Collapse: 7% Attrition: 24% MLB: 70%
Comparables: Jason Kipnis, Ryan Adams, Devon Travis

Despite his youth and nearly-faded prospect sheen, Dilson Herrera hasn't shown much promise in recent years and his increasing lack of plate discipline doesn't give much hope that he'll rediscover any of that magic—not only was his strikeout rate obscene in his small sample with the Reds, but it has gone the wrong direction in each of his last three seasons in Triple-A. He'll play for a major-league team when there are injuries, but it's entirely possible that the 103 plate appearances with the Mets in 2015 are going to go down as his career high.

YEAR	TEAM	LVL	AGE	PA	DRC+	VORP	BABIP	BRR	FRAA	WARP
2016	LVG	AAA	22	389	97	11.0	.313	0.5	2B(75): -4.7	-0.1
2016	LOU	AAA	22	80	115	6.4	.306	0.1	2B(16): -0.1	0.2
2017	LOU	AAA	23	265	90	4.3	.322	-1.7	2B(55): 0.8, 3B(3): 0.2	0.0
2018	DAY	A+	24	92	118	4.7	.365	1.0	2B(19): 3.1	0.7
2018	LOU	AAA	24	208	137	10.1	.372	-2.8	2B(35): 0.6, 3B(11): 1.7	1.1
2018	CIN	MLB	24	97	74	-0.4	.256	-0.6	2B(13): -0.7, LF(11): -0.2	-0.2
2019	NYN	MLB	25	251	75	0.0	.271	-0.5	2B 0, 3B 1	0.1

Dilson Herrera, continued

Batted Ball Distribution

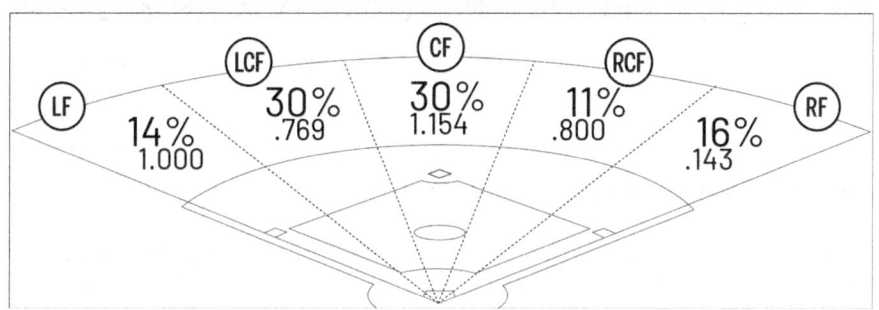

Strike Zone vs LHP   **Strike Zone vs RHP**

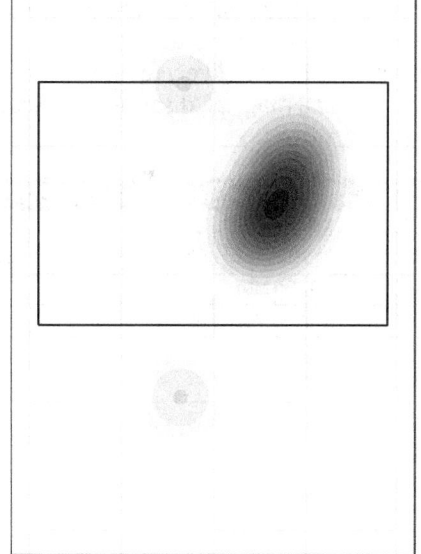

Juan Lagares CF

Born: 03/17/89 Age: 30 Bats: R Throws: R
Height: 6'1" Weight: 215 Origin: International Free Agent, 2006

YEAR	TEAM	LVL	AGE	PA	R	2B	3B	HR	RBI	BB	K	SB	CS	AVG/OBP/SLG
2016	NYN	MLB	27	160	15	7	2	3	9	11	27	4	2	.239/.301/.380
2017	NYN	MLB	28	272	37	16	2	3	15	14	56	7	3	.250/.296/.365
2018	NYN	MLB	29	64	9	1	1	0	6	3	9	3	1	.339/.375/.390
2019	NYN	MLB	30	111	12	5	1	2	11	8	22	3	1	.248/.306/.376

Breakout: 4%   Improve: 41%   Collapse: 9%   Attrition: 8%   MLB: 95%
Comparables: Steve Finley, Harry Walker, Ted Uhlaender

Over the past three years, Lagares has been injured often enough that you'd think the Mets are staging a revival of *Brigadoon* in the middle of their outfield. The team's fleet-of-foot and utterly platoonable center fielder only shows up once in a while, and with conditions. The thumb and oblique injuries that dogged him in '16 and '17 didn't recur, but he tore a toe ligament in May that required season-ending surgery. His sizzling start to the season proved that he can still be a valuable commodity when he takes the field, capable of providing excellent defense and the occasional run of hot hitting against lefties. But you're probably about as likely to find him spending regular time in the outfield as you are to find a magical, disappearing Scottish village, which is to say not very likely at all.

YEAR	TEAM	LVL	AGE	PA	DRC+	VORP	BABIP	BRR	FRAA	WARP
2016	NYN	MLB	27	160	84	2.4	.274	0.1	CF(68): 1.4, RF(2): 0.1	0.4
2017	NYN	MLB	28	272	69	3.3	.309	1.9	CF(85): 6.2	0.7
2018	NYN	MLB	29	64	88	5.7	.392	1.0	CF(20): 1.5	0.4
2019	NYN	MLB	30	111	83	2.5	.282	0.1	CF 0	0.2

Juan Lagares, continued

Batted Ball Distribution

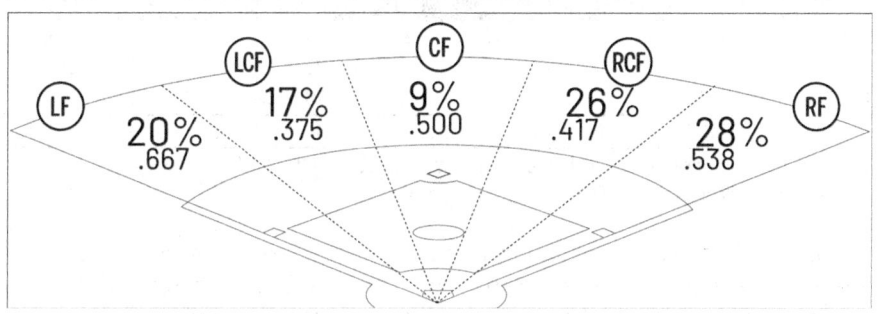

Strike Zone vs LHP   **Strike Zone vs RHP**

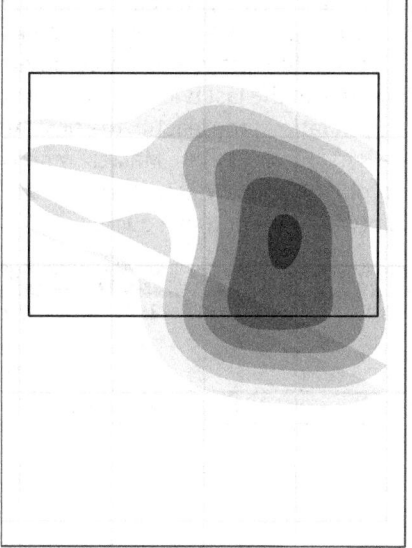

Jed Lowrie 2B

Born: 04/17/84 Age: 35 Bats: B Throws: R
Height: 6'0" Weight: 180 Origin: Round 1, 2005 Draft (#45 overall)

YEAR	TEAM	LVL	AGE	PA	R	2B	3B	HR	RBI	BB	K	SB	CS	AVG/OBP/SLG
2016	OAK	MLB	32	369	30	12	1	2	27	26	65	0	0	.263/.314/.322
2017	OAK	MLB	33	645	86	49	3	14	69	73	100	0	1	.277/.360/.448
2018	OAK	MLB	34	680	78	37	1	23	99	78	128	0	0	.267/.353/.448
2019	NYN	MLB	35	462	49	26	2	10	52	46	83	0	0	.271/.346/.417

Breakout: 0% Improve: 23% Collapse: 20% Attrition: 12% MLB: 81%
Comparables: Orlando Hudson, Frankie Frisch, Ian Kinsler

We opened last year's comment by pointing out that Lowrie was meant to be the A's placeholder for Franklin Barreto until he went out and had his best performance in years. Well, folks, he did it again, this time sending a few more balls over the wall that in 2017 had been doubles, resulting in the second-best WARP of his career, behind his 2012 season in Houston. PECOTA looks at Lowrie's age and sees a cliff coming, but that's what PECOTA said last winter, too. It's just as easy to see an injury-hastened fade into oblivion as it is to see him putting up above-average hitting lines with adequate defense until he's 40. "Give us a fun fact to end the comment!" you say? You got it. Lowrie attempted one steal in the last two years despite 1,325 plate appearances, easily the highest ratio in the league; the next-highest PA totals with zero or one attempts are Ryon Healy (1,129), Maikel Franco (1,088), Robinson Cano (996), Mark Trumbo (961) and Victor Martinez (943), all of whom have a listed weight at least 30 pounds higher than Lowrie.

YEAR	TEAM	LVL	AGE	PA	DRC+	VORP	BABIP	BRR	FRAA	WARP
2016	OAK	MLB	32	369	84	-2.9	.316	-1.1	2B(82): 2.0, SS(2): 0.0	0.4
2017	OAK	MLB	33	645	114	25.6	.314	-2.4	2B(136): -3.5, 3B(1): 0.2	2.4
2018	OAK	MLB	34	680	126	38.5	.304	-3.0	2B(136): -0.4, 3B(14): -0.5	3.9
2019	NYN	MLB	35	462	109	17.0	.313	-0.9	3B -4, 2B -1	1.3

Jed Lowrie, continued

Batted Ball Distribution

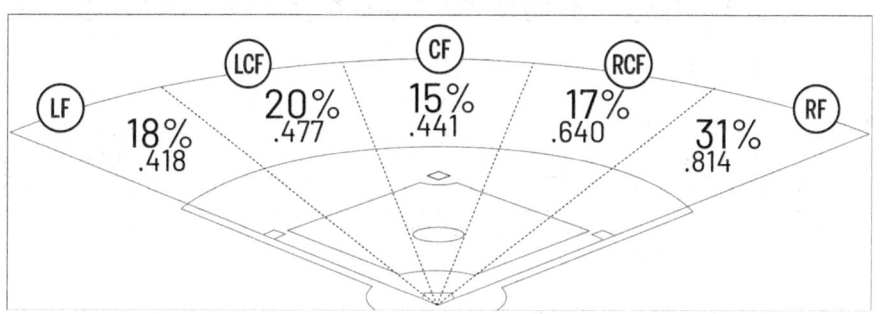

Strike Zone vs LHP　　　**Strike Zone vs RHP**

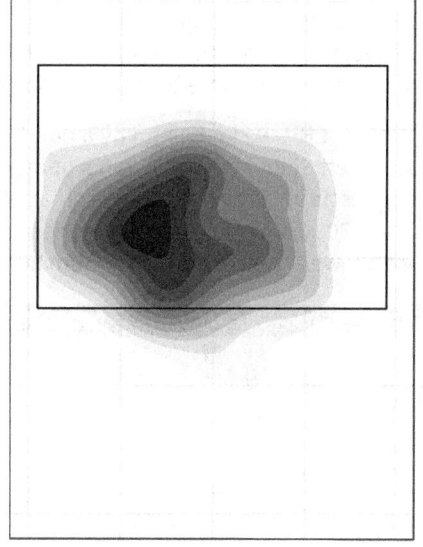

Jeff McNeil 2B
Born: 04/08/92 Age: 27 Bats: L Throws: R
Height: 6'1" Weight: 195 Origin: Round 12, 2013 Draft (#356 overall)

YEAR	TEAM	LVL	AGE	PA	R	2B	3B	HR	RBI	BB	K	SB	CS	AVG/OBP/SLG
2017	SLU	A+	25	116	13	7	0	3	15	7	19	2	2	.324/.388/.476
2017	LVG	AAA	25	78	12	5	0	1	6	3	10	2	0	.254/.295/.366
2018	BIN	AA	26	241	49	16	3	14	43	22	23	3	0	.327/.402/.626
2018	LVG	AAA	26	143	23	10	2	5	28	14	19	3	0	.368/.427/.600
2018	NYN	MLB	26	248	35	11	6	3	19	14	24	7	1	.329/.381/.471
2019	NYN	MLB	27	558	62	27	6	13	64	40	86	8	2	.279/.339/.434

Breakout: 5% Improve: 49% Collapse: 7% Attrition: 30% MLB: 95%
Comparables: Jordany Valdespin, Rob Refsnyder, Justin Turner

It wasn't supposed to be like this. A low-round draft pick, almost always old for his league, owner of just one preternatural skill: the ability to get hits. McNeil has been one of those players defined by his imperfections, including but not limited to a lack of pedigree and no ideal place to stand on the diamond except the batter's box. Year after year, McNeil put up big minor league numbers, until even a Mets organization who'd shown precious little faith in him as a big-leaguer was forced to give him a shot. McNeil took his opportunity and was as good a hitter on a rate basis as anyone on the Mets.

Here at BP, we know him by a number that isn't even on his jersey: *Six*. Coined by Jarrett Seidler, it refers to his opinion on McNeil's projected role in the big leagues as an above-average regular. McNeil may well be a first-division starter and a .300 hitter. After how good he's looked over the past couple of years, we're not allowed to be surprised by him anymore. Six has blossomed.

YEAR	TEAM	LVL	AGE	PA	DRC+	VORP	BABIP	BRR	FRAA	WARP
2017	SLU	A+	25	116	155	7.2	.373	-0.6	2B(18): -1.5, 3B(4): -0.3	0.4
2017	LVG	AAA	25	78	69	0.4	.274	1.0	2B(17): 0.2, 3B(1): 0.6	0.1
2018	BIN	AA	26	241	175	31.4	.316	1.7	2B(47): 3.9, 3B(9): -0.6	2.9
2018	LVG	AAA	26	143	156	15.4	.394	0.4	2B(24): -3.3, 3B(3): -0.1	0.9
2018	NYN	MLB	26	248	119	24.1	.359	0.8	2B(54): -2.6, 3B(4): 0.3	1.2
2019	NYN	MLB	27	558	112	26.2	.311	0.9	LF 2, 3B 0	2.8

Jeff McNeil, continued

Batted Ball Distribution

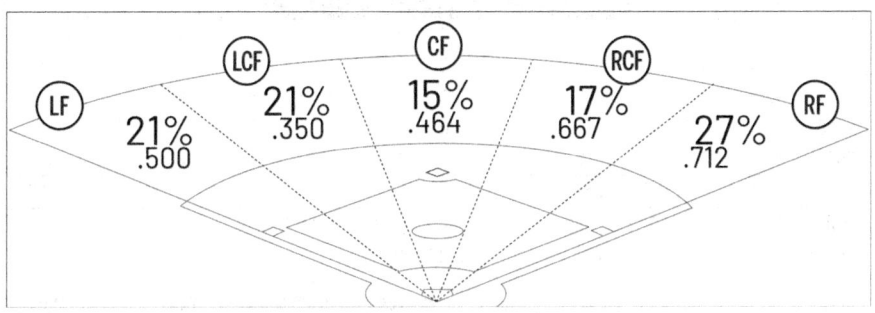

Strike Zone vs LHP

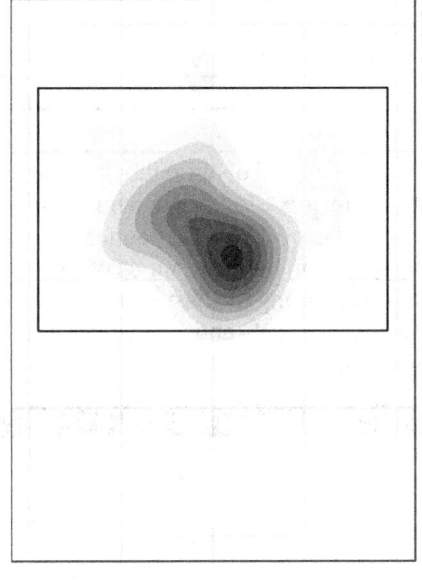

Strike Zone vs RHP

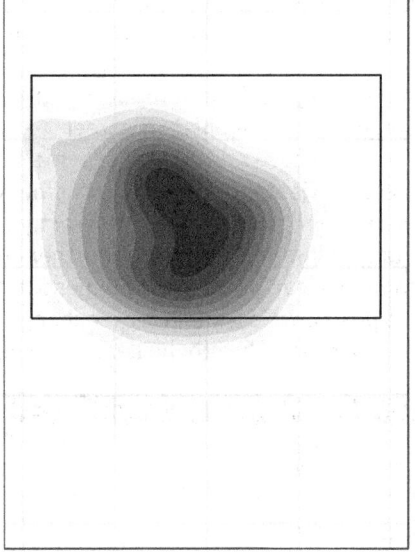

Devin Mesoraco C

Born: 06/19/88 Age: 31 Bats: R Throws: R
Height: 6'1" Weight: 229 Origin: Round 1, 2007 Draft (#15 overall)

YEAR	TEAM	LVL	AGE	PA	R	2B	3B	HR	RBI	BB	K	SB	CS	AVG/OBP/SLG
2016	CIN	MLB	28	55	2	1	0	0	1	5	10	0	1	.140/.218/.160
2017	PEN	AA	29	55	4	1	0	1	3	6	10	0	0	.170/.291/.255
2017	CIN	MLB	29	165	17	5	1	6	14	18	38	1	0	.213/.321/.390
2018	CIN	MLB	30	45	1	2	0	1	3	2	10	0	0	.220/.289/.341
2018	NYN	MLB	30	229	23	8	0	10	30	23	42	0	0	.222/.306/.409
2019	NYN	MLB	31	251	28	10	1	7	28	24	52	1	0	.235/.322/.383

Breakout: 1% Improve: 35% Collapse: 19% Attrition: 17% MLB: 95%
Comparables: Ryan Doumit, Miguel Montero, Brian McCann

Nothing beats a good challenge trade where both players improve after a move. While Matt Harvey's semi-renaissance was the bigger story of the Mets and Reds' headache-swap, Mesoraco had the second-best season of his career simply by staying moderately healthy. Sure, the multiple surgeries that derailed his career appear to have robbed him of some of his power and all of his reliability, but Mesoraco is still, put simply, a catcher with some pop. His defensive numbers were never good but now are exactly what you'd expect from someone with his litany of injuries, and yet the further out he gets from his latest surgery, the more one can dream on a slugger who was once among the best in the game at his position. He'll find another change of scenery in 2019, and if it comes with another run of health, he'll be an excellent value.

YEAR	TEAM	P. COUNT	FRM RUNS	BLK RUNS	THRW RUNS	TOT RUNS
2016	CIN	2035	-1.2	-0.2	0.0	-1.6
2017	CIN	5242	-5.5	1.6	-0.4	-4.9
2017	PEN	1408	-0.5	0.0	0.0	-0.7
2018	CIN	1378	-1.2	0.5	0.0	-0.7
2018	NYN	7897	-6.2	0.0	-0.4	-6.7
2019	NYN	9117	-8.6	0.6	-0.3	-8.4

YEAR	TEAM	LVL	AGE	PA	DRC+	VORP	BABIP	BRR	FRAA	WARP
2016	CIN	MLB	28	55	67	-4.6	.175	-0.6	C(13): -1.8	-0.2
2017	PEN	AA	29	55	74	-0.3	.194	-0.6	C(11): -0.5	-0.2
2017	CIN	MLB	29	165	89	5.2	.245	-0.8	C(40): -3.0	0.2
2018	CIN	MLB	30	45	97	-0.5	.267	-0.1	C(10): -0.7, 1B(1): 0.0	0.1
2018	NYN	MLB	30	229	99	8.8	.230	0.2	C(57): -6.6	0.4
2019	NYN	MLB	31	251	95	9.5	.279	-0.3	C -8, 1B 0	0.2

Devin Mesoraco, continued

Batted Ball Distribution

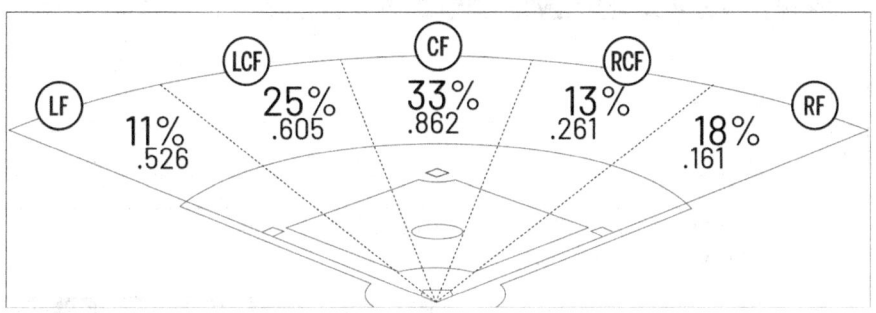

Strike Zone vs LHP **Strike Zone vs RHP**

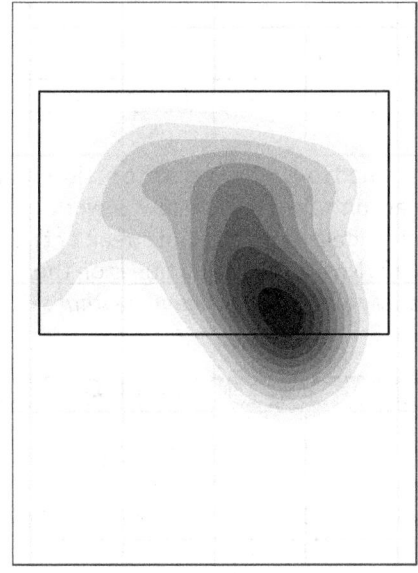 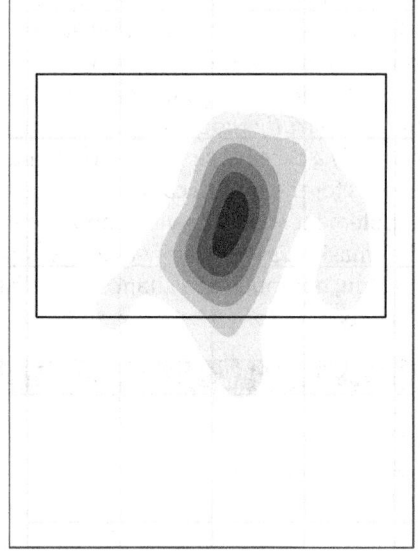

New York Mets 2019

Tomas Nido C
Born: 04/12/94   Age: 25   Bats: R   Throws: R
Height: 6'0"   Weight: 210   Origin: Round 8, 2012 Draft (#260 overall)

YEAR	TEAM	LVL	AGE	PA	R	2B	3B	HR	RBI	BB	K	SB	CS	AVG/OBP/SLG
2016	SLU	A+	22	370	38	23	2	7	46	19	42	0	1	.320/.357/.459
2017	BIN	AA	23	404	41	19	1	8	60	30	63	0	0	.232/.287/.354
2017	NYN	MLB	23	10	0	1	0	0	3	0	2	0	0	.300/.300/.400
2018	BIN	AA	24	228	23	18	1	5	30	7	36	0	0	.274/.298/.437
2018	NYN	MLB	24	90	10	3	0	1	9	4	27	0	0	.167/.200/.238
2019	NYN	MLB	25	62	7	3	0	2	7	5	15	0	0	.250/.323/.411

Breakout: 17%   Improve: 33%   Collapse: 1%   Attrition: 22%   MLB: 40%
Comparables: Tony Cruz, James McCann, Kyle Farmer

The truth is a continuum, living somewhere between two points of objective reference. For example, in 2016, Nido was a minor-league batting champion, but in 2018 he hit .167 over 34 major-league games. Nearly every statistical possibility lies somewhere between those two goalposts, but here's the *truth*: Nido is almost certainly a defense-first backup catcher destined to flirt between the majors and minors for the next decade. He has solid bat control and a little raw power to supplement solid receiving chops—enough to help him ride a hot streak or two that masks his well-below-average approach. No future batting title is on the horizon, nor much of a chance to whiff his way out of the big leagues—*that's* the veracity of Nido.

YEAR	TEAM	P. COUNT	FRM RUNS	BLK RUNS	THRW RUNS	TOT RUNS
2017	BIN	10148	27.4	2.3	0.6	30.8
2017	NYN	379	0.1	0.3	0.0	1.7
2018	BIN	6337	7.7	0.0	0.5	8.2
2018	LVG	727	0.4	-0.1	0.0	0.2
2018	NYN	3444	3.5	-0.1	0.0	3.3
2019	NYN	2357	2.4	0.2	0.0	2.6

YEAR	TEAM	LVL	AGE	PA	DRC+	VORP	BABIP	BRR	FRAA	WARP
2016	SLU	A+	22	370	142	27.8	.344	-2.4	C(88): 4.8	2.7
2017	BIN	AA	23	404	70	4.5	.255	2.4	C(85): 28.4	2.9
2017	NYN	MLB	23	10	89	0.2	.375	-0.1	C(3): 0.3	0.1
2018	BIN	AA	24	228	111	6.1	.303	-2.0	C(48): 8.5	1.6
2018	NYN	MLB	24	90	58	-3.7	.224	0.2	C(30): 3.4	0.3
2019	NYN	MLB	25	62	84	1.6	.284	-0.1	C 2	0.4

Tomas Nido, continued

Batted Ball Distribution

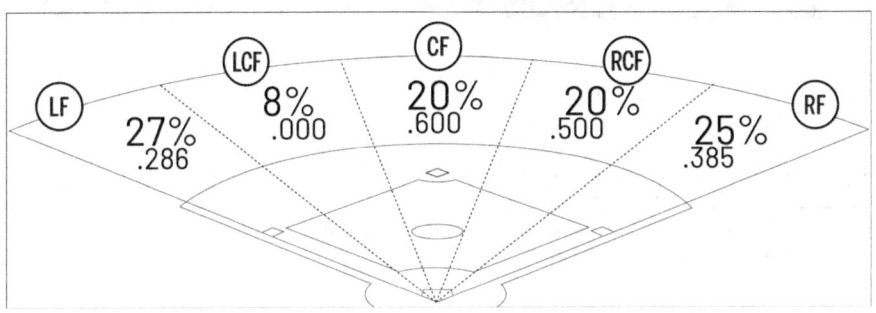

Strike Zone vs LHP

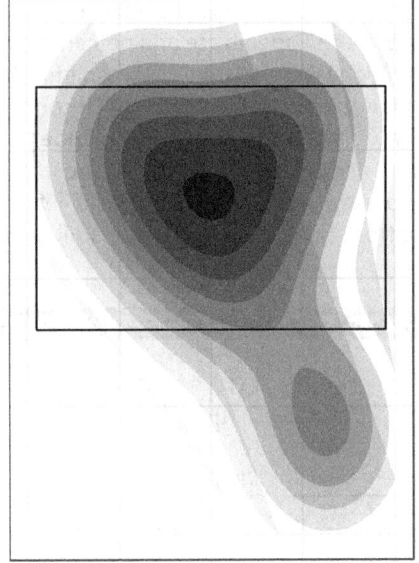

Strike Zone vs RHP

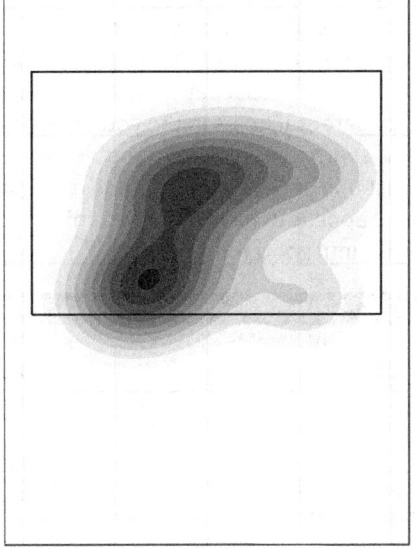

Brandon Nimmo OF

Born: 03/27/93 Age: 26 Bats: L Throws: R
Height: 6'3" Weight: 207 Origin: Round 1, 2011 Draft (#13 overall)

YEAR	TEAM	LVL	AGE	PA	R	2B	3B	HR	RBI	BB	K	SB	CS	AVG/OBP/SLG
2016	LVG	AAA	23	444	72	25	8	11	61	46	73	7	8	.352/.423/.541
2016	NYN	MLB	23	80	12	1	0	1	6	6	20	0	0	.274/.338/.329
2017	LVG	AAA	24	198	23	12	1	3	17	33	49	0	0	.227/.364/.368
2017	NYN	MLB	24	215	26	11	1	5	21	33	60	2	0	.260/.379/.418
2018	NYN	MLB	25	535	77	28	8	17	47	80	140	9	6	.263/.404/.483
2019	NYN	MLB	26	631	83	27	6	17	65	73	162	7	4	.246/.349/.413

Breakout: 8%   Improve: 47%   Collapse: 6%   Attrition: 9%   MLB: 95%
Comparables: Jorge Soler, Stephen Piscotty, Derek Dietrich

For some, patience can feel like a chore. For Nimmo, it appears to be second nature. Smile and wait through the slow burn of the Mets' minor-league system. Smile and wait until the team can no longer deny your incredible on-base skills. Smile and wait for the perfect pitch, then drive it into the gap. Nimmo's practiced approach at the plate put him in the top 20 hitters in baseball in esoteric stats like strikes thrown, pitches per plate appearance and percentage of pitches taken without swinging. You'd think he were passive if it wasn't for the hustle on the basepaths and his penchant for attacking the first pitch. Of course there are still holes in the youngster's game: he's not much of a center fielder and southpaws give him trouble, but there's a chance he can still improve in at least one of those areas. In the meantime, during his plate appearances, Mets fans appear to have learned a thing or two from Nimmo—they tend to smile and wait until good things happen.

YEAR	TEAM	LVL	AGE	PA	DRC+	VORP	BABIP	BRR	FRAA	WARP
2016	LVG	AAA	23	444	149	35.3	.411	2.8	CF(65): 2.6, LF(23): 1.6	3.6
2016	NYN	MLB	23	80	84	2.0	.365	-0.4	LF(13): -0.2, RF(7): -0.1	0.0
2017	LVG	AAA	24	198	96	5.4	.306	-1.0	CF(31): -4.8, RF(12): 2.2	-0.1
2017	NYN	MLB	24	215	92	12.1	.360	-0.9	LF(32): 3.0, CF(12): 0.5	0.6
2018	NYN	MLB	25	535	123	56.5	.351	5.1	RF(62): 0.1, CF(44): -0.9	3.6
2019	NYN	MLB	26	631	112	36.0	.317	-0.4	CF -7, RF 1	2.7

Brandon Nimmo, continued

Batted Ball Distribution

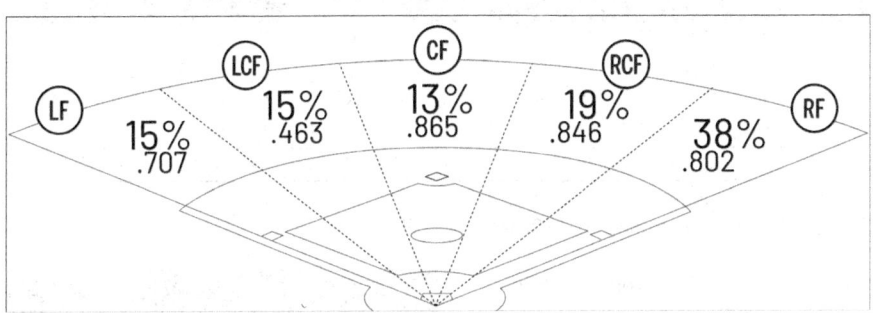

Strike Zone vs LHP   **Strike Zone vs RHP**

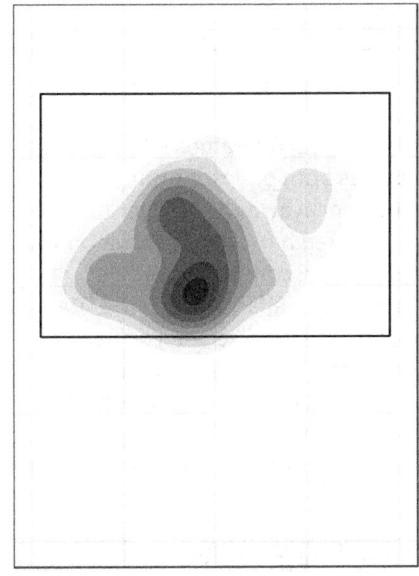
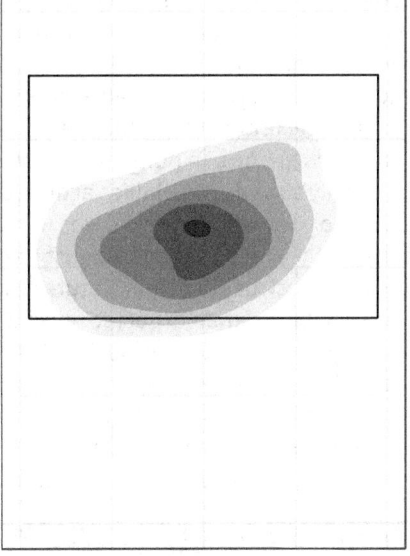

Wilson Ramos C

Born: 08/10/87 Age: 31 Bats: R Throws: R
Height: 6'1" Weight: 245 Origin: International Free Agent, 2004

YEAR	TEAM	LVL	AGE	PA	R	2B	3B	HR	RBI	BB	K	SB	CS	AVG/OBP/SLG
2016	WAS	MLB	28	523	58	25	0	22	80	35	79	0	0	.307/.354/.496
2017	TBA	MLB	29	224	19	6	0	11	35	10	36	0	0	.260/.290/.447
2018	TBA	MLB	30	315	30	14	0	14	53	22	61	0	0	.297/.346/.488
2018	PHI	MLB	30	101	9	8	1	1	17	10	19	0	0	.337/.396/.483
2019	NYN	MLB	31	413	47	17	1	14	52	31	73	0	0	.265/.324/.427

Breakout: 2% Improve: 28% Collapse: 28% Attrition: 18% MLB: 92%
Comparables: Ramon Hernandez, Harry Danning, Matt Wieters

YEAR	TEAM	P. COUNT	FRM RUNS	BLK RUNS	THRW RUNS	TOT RUNS
2016	WAS	17715	10.7	-1.2	1.6	11.4
2017	DUR	799	0.3	0.1	0.0	0.3
2017	TBA	8203	1.4	-3.9	-0.8	-4.1
2018	TBA	9850	0.2	0.3	-0.2	0.6
2018	PHI	3106	0.1	-0.3	0.2	0.3
2019	NYN	14522	2.0	-2.2	0.1	-0.1

If the August and September Phillies were a quilt, Ramos could be thought of as the patch sewn in just left-of-center, prettily obscuring the hole that still exists behind it but not quite perfectly blending in. The Phils had rather ably made it to late July with a backstop tandem of Jorge Alfaro and Andrew Knapp, but as the latter grew increasingly untenable, a non-waiver deadline move like Ramos felt warranted. Really, it was one of a number of moves that was both philosophically and materially sound: The Phillies acquired Ramos on layaway at a player-to-be-named-or-cash discount—he was nursing an injured hamstring and was known to be on the shelf until mid-August—and his expiring contract meant he wouldn't obstruct the club's future plans to ride with Alfaro. For a while, Ramos was even better than expected, even if he probably could've been declared statuary on account of his obviously stiff lower body. But then, like the rest of the Phillies, his game went in the tank over the final two weeks, sucked into an eminently forgettable void that, mercifully, few of us will remember for long. That said, he traded one void for another by signing with the Mets in December to lead their group of almost-catchers.

YEAR	TEAM	LVL	AGE	PA	DRC+	VORP	BABIP	BRR	FRAA	WARP
2016	WAS	MLB	28	523	121	43.2	.327	-4.3	C(128): 10.0	4.5
2017	TBA	MLB	29	224	101	4.1	.262	-3.4	C(62): -3.1	0.5
2018	TBA	MLB	30	315	121	15.9	.335	-4.4	C(73): -0.8	1.8
2018	PHI	MLB	30	101	123	8.3	.408	-2.6	C(23): 0.0	0.5
2019	NYN	MLB	31	413	108	19.8	.297	-0.7	C -3	1.8

Wilson Ramos, continued

Batted Ball Distribution

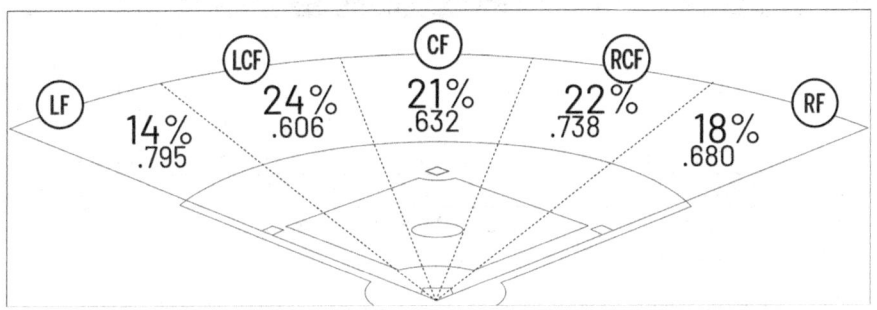

Strike Zone vs LHP

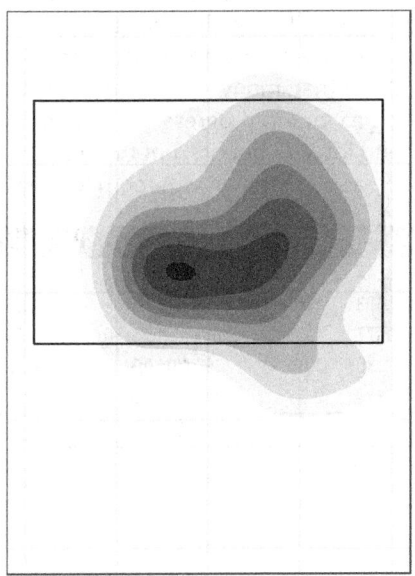

Strike Zone vs RHP

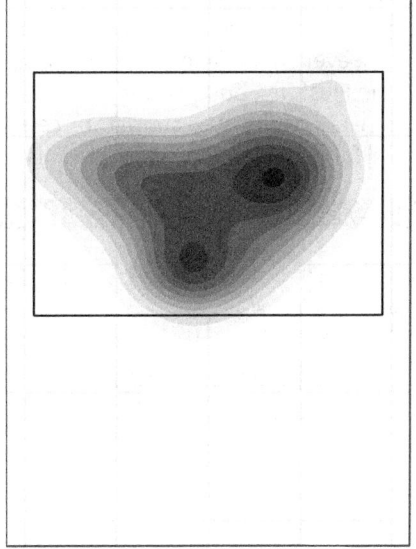

Amed Rosario SS

Born: 11/20/95 Age: 23 Bats: R Throws: R
Height: 6'2" Weight: 189 Origin: International Free Agent, 2012

YEAR	TEAM	LVL	AGE	PA	R	2B	3B	HR	RBI	BB	K	SB	CS	AVG/OBP/SLG
2016	SLU	A+	20	290	27	10	8	3	40	21	36	13	6	.309/.359/.442
2016	BIN	AA	20	237	38	14	5	2	31	19	51	6	2	.341/.392/.481
2017	LVG	AAA	21	425	66	19	7	7	58	23	67	19	6	.328/.367/.466
2017	NYN	MLB	21	170	16	4	4	4	10	3	49	7	3	.248/.271/.394
2018	NYN	MLB	22	592	76	26	8	9	51	29	119	24	11	.256/.295/.381
2019	NYN	MLB	23	619	78	23	7	13	55	35	125	22	9	.253/.299/.385

Breakout: 29% Improve: 63% Collapse: 15% Attrition: 15% MLB: 93%
Comparables: Orlando Arcia, Hanley Ramirez, Ketel Marte

The start to this past summer was cruel to Rosario's bat, but this electric youngster finally started to put his offensive tools together in August and September. Finally given regular playing time in the second half, Rosario started to look more comfortable at the plate. His plus contact skills started to translate into hits and his speed played up on the basepaths, though his swing-happy approach still kept his on-base percentage depressed. He's no finished product by far, even in the field where he's a sight better than many who've manned the dirt in Flushing, but not elite. It's tough being a work-in-progress in a league where almost half the shortstops can contend for MVP honors, but there's no need for discouragement—Rosario is already a solid regular with room to grow.

YEAR	TEAM	LVL	AGE	PA	DRC+	VORP	BABIP	BRR	FRAA	WARP
2016	SLU	A+	20	290	147	24.0	.345	0.5	SS(60): -0.4	1.9
2016	BIN	AA	20	237	113	20.9	.433	1.7	SS(53): -4.9	0.6
2017	LVG	AAA	21	425	116	30.2	.377	1.4	SS(88): 2.0, 3B(6): -0.2	2.5
2017	NYN	MLB	21	170	69	0.6	.330	1.0	SS(45): -0.3	0.2
2018	NYN	MLB	22	592	83	22.2	.310	2.8	SS(146): -6.6	1.0
2019	NYN	MLB	23	619	88	18.3	.299	2.0	SS -4	1.2

Amed Rosario, continued

Batted Ball Distribution

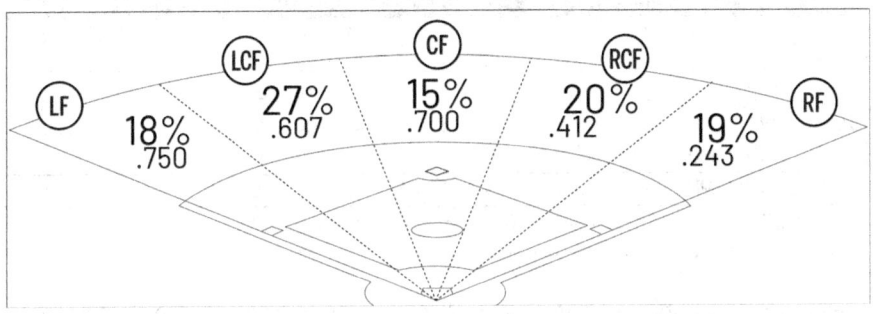

Strike Zone vs LHP **Strike Zone vs RHP**

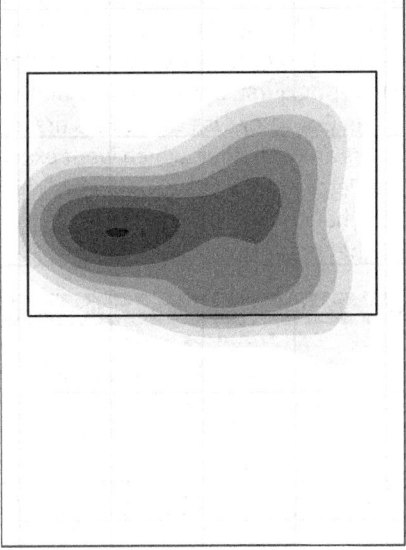

New York Mets 2019

Dominic Smith 1B
Born: 06/15/95 Age: 24 Bats: L Throws: L
Height: 6'0" Weight: 239 Origin: Round 1, 2013 Draft (#11 overall)

YEAR	TEAM	LVL	AGE	PA	R	2B	3B	HR	RBI	BB	K	SB	CS	AVG/OBP/SLG
2016	BIN	AA	21	542	64	29	2	14	91	50	74	2	1	.302/.367/.457
2017	LVG	AAA	22	500	77	34	2	16	76	39	87	1	1	.330/.386/.519
2017	NYN	MLB	22	183	17	6	0	9	26	14	49	0	0	.198/.262/.395
2018	LVG	AAA	23	375	52	21	1	6	41	34	76	3	0	.258/.328/.380
2018	NYN	MLB	23	149	14	11	1	5	11	4	47	0	0	.224/.255/.420
2019	NYN	MLB	24	173	18	9	1	5	20	11	42	0	0	.244/.295/.406

Breakout: 8% Improve: 38% Collapse: 0% Attrition: 26% MLB: 52%
Comparables: Chris Marrero, Kendrys Morales, Joey Votto

Previous comments in this very Annual pegged Smith as an ill fit for first base; his bat-to-ball abilities always seemed better suited for a soft-handed second baseman or speedy left fielder. But 2018 was another year of the former top prospect's surprise conversion into all-or-nothing home run hitter. Instead of reaching base and driving the ball into the gap, he's now a longball hunter, and instead of being a *better* offensive player he's just a *different* one. Due to a logjam of cold-corner-only bats to start this past season, Smith did a bit of wandering. First, back to Vegas where there was nothing left to prove because Adrian Gonzalez was the team's first choice at the position. Later, the Mets tried him as an outfielder, which went exactly as poorly as everyone expected. Now that Peter Alonso has zoomed past him on the organization depth chart, Smith's best chance to establish himself in the majors might require a journey to another organization.

YEAR	TEAM	LVL	AGE	PA	DRC+	VORP	BABIP	BRR	FRAA	WARP
2016	BIN	AA	21	542	118	17.6	.329	-5.3	1B(106): 1.1	0.3
2017	LVG	AAA	22	500	130	22.5	.380	-2.4	1B(107): 6.6	2.1
2017	NYN	MLB	22	183	80	-3.4	.218	0.3	1B(46): -5.5	-0.7
2018	LVG	AAA	23	375	81	3.6	.315	1.9	1B(53): 6.5, LF(22): -0.2	0.5
2018	NYN	MLB	23	149	77	1.0	.297	0.3	1B(28): -0.5, LF(13): -1.9	-0.4
2019	NYN	MLB	24	173	88	1.7	.290	-0.3	1B 1	0.2

Dominic Smith, continued

Batted Ball Distribution

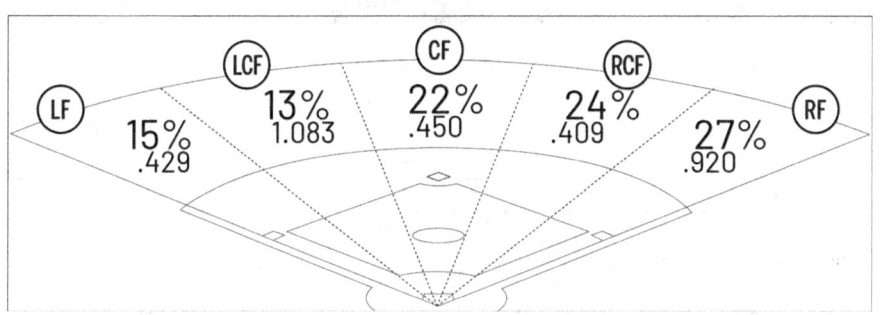

Strike Zone vs LHP   **Strike Zone vs RHP**

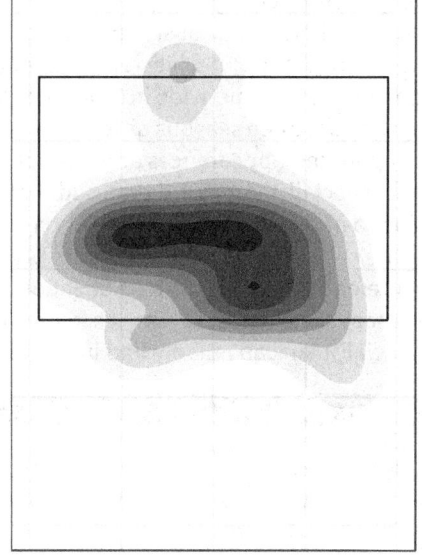

New York Mets 2019

Luis Avilan LHP
Born: 07/19/89 Age: 29 Bats: L Throws: L
Height: 6'2" Weight: 220 Origin: International Free Agent, 2005

YEAR	TEAM	LVL	AGE	W	L	SV	G	GS	IP	H	HR	BB/9	K/9	K	GB%	BABIP
2016	OKL	AAA	26	0	3	4	33	0	34	35	3	4.2	9.8	37	49%	.337
2016	LAN	MLB	26	3	0	0	27	0	19²	12	0	4.6	12.8	28	55%	.286
2017	LAN	MLB	27	2	3	0	61	0	46	42	2	4.3	10.2	52	56%	.342
2018	CHA	MLB	28	2	1	2	58	0	39²	40	2	3.2	10.4	46	37%	.352
2018	PHI	MLB	28	0	0	0	12	0	5²	4	1	6.4	7.9	5	38%	.200
2019	NYN	MLB	29	2	1	1	39	0	41	35	5	4.3	10.3	47	44%	.304

Breakout: 31% Improve: 46% Collapse: 24% Attrition: 20% MLB: 92%
Comparables: Brandon League, Jared Burton, Bobby Parnell

There are a number of side effects to the new wave of pitcher management. Most have thus far simply been growing pains, the products of stirring a tablespoon of discomfort into the drink of expectation and predictability that had come to define the starter-setup-closer paradigm of the modern game. The past twenty years gently pushed those walls out, slowly, with match-up play and one-batter specialists finding more frequent—if still necessarily brief—time in the spotlight. But while relief appearances of one single batter faced rose above 1,400 league-wide in 2015, they have dropped back below 1,200 in each of the past three seasons as teams lean toward stretch types who can handle wraparound appearances and multiple innings. All of this brings us to Avilan: A lefty specialist in a world that, suddenly, teams might lean on less and less. How does a pitcher of limited utility fit on staffs that might regularly ask for more and more coverage from their relievers? Avilan, to his credit, is good at what he does. A premature end would be a plight of circumstance, not ability. But as the game reshapes itself around him, it's fair to wonder how much longer Avilan and his specialist kin can reliably find homes in Major League bullpens.

YEAR	TEAM	LVL	AGE	WHIP	ERA	DRA	WARP	MPH	FB%	WHF	CSP
2016	OKL	AAA	26	1.50	4.24	3.07	0.7				
2016	LAN	MLB	26	1.12	3.20	3.07	0.4	94.4	45.7	18.6	37.4
2017	LAN	MLB	27	1.39	2.93	3.33	0.9	94.3	41.7	15.1	33
2018	CHA	MLB	28	1.36	3.86	4.83	0.0	92.3	35.5	10.8	42.3
2018	PHI	MLB	28	1.41	3.18	5.26	0.0	91.9	41.8	13.3	43.6
2019	NYN	MLB	29	1.32	4.07	4.69	0.1	92.7	39.4	13.5	38

Luis Avilan, continued

Pitch Shape vs LHH

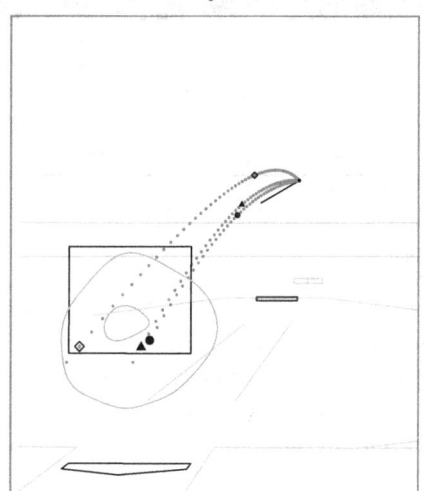

Pitch Shape vs RHH

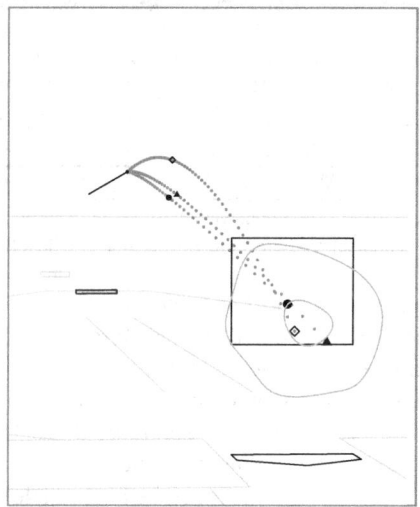

Type	Frequency	Velocity	H Movement	V Movement
● Fastball	36.2%	90.5 [94]	13.4 [69]	-20.2 [86]
□ Sinker				
+ Cutter				
▲ Changeup	46.1%	82.2 [88]	10.5 [104]	-31.4 [88]
× Splitter				
▽ Slider				
◇ Curveball	17.7%	71.2 [73]	-9.9 [109]	-56.2 [82]
⊕ Slow Curveball				
✳ Knuckleball				
▼ Screwball				

Tyler Bashlor RHP

Born: 04/16/93 Age: 26 Bats: R Throws: R
Height: 6'0" Weight: 195 Origin: Round 11, 2013 Draft (#326 overall)

YEAR	TEAM	LVL	AGE	W	L	SV	G	GS	IP	H	HR	BB/9	K/9	K	GB%	BABIP
2016	COL	A	23	4	2	3	34	0	50^1	35	2	5.0	12.2	68	47%	.292
2017	SLU	A+	24	2	2	10	34	0	35	33	1	5.4	15.7	61	39%	.438
2017	BIN	AA	24	1	0	3	12	0	14^2	7	0	2.5	14.1	23	41%	.259
2018	BIN	AA	25	0	3	7	20	0	24	14	2	4.5	11.2	30	30%	.235
2018	NYN	MLB	25	0	3	0	24	0	32	26	6	3.4	7.0	25	32%	.225
2019	NYN	MLB	26	2	2	0	41	0	43	40	7	5.2	10.1	49	37%	.292

Breakout: 17% Improve: 24% Collapse: 13% Attrition: 21% MLB: 47%
Comparables: Pedro Strop, David Carpenter, Brad Boxberger

Bashlor, a late-developing strikeout artist, was bumped from Double-A to the majors in June due to the Mets' woeful bullpen situation. Already old for the Eastern League, this fireballer's shift to Queens wasn't nearly as smooth as either party would've liked. Command was once an issue for Bashlor, but in the majors he didn't have an issue there; the problem was mainly that major-league hitters did not flail at his slider as much as he was used to in the upper minors. In September, however, he looked a lot more like the dominant reliever that Met prospect hounds have dreamed on—he whiffed 10 of the 30 batters he faced and held opposing hitters to a .154 batting average. With his raw stuff, he'll certainly get another handful of chances to work his way into a leveraged role, even in an improved 2019 bullpen.

YEAR	TEAM	LVL	AGE	WHIP	ERA	DRA	WARP	MPH	FB%	WHF	CSP
2016	COL	A	23	1.25	2.50	2.73	1.2				
2017	SLU	A+	24	1.54	4.89	2.24	1.1				
2017	BIN	AA	24	0.75	0.00	2.34	0.4				
2018	BIN	AA	25	1.08	2.62	3.14	0.5				
2018	NYN	MLB	25	1.19	4.22	5.68	-0.3	98.3	68.9	11.9	45.7
2019	NYN	MLB	26	1.49	5.37	5.52	-0.4	97.9	70.1	12.1	46.5

Tyler Bashlor, continued

Pitch Shape vs LHH

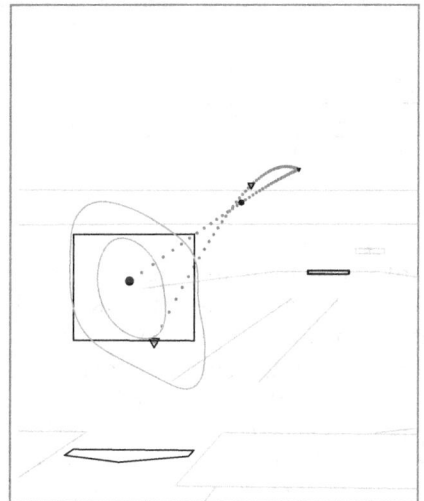

Pitch Shape vs RHH

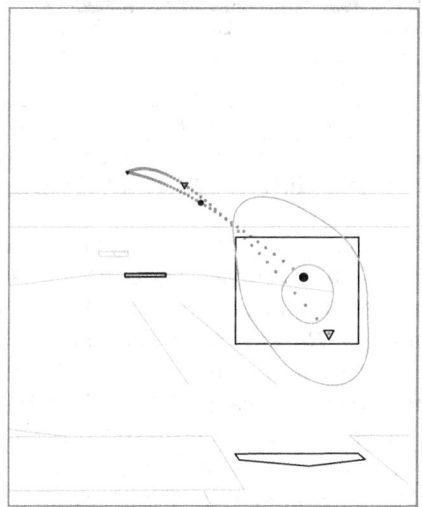

Type	Frequency	Velocity	H Movement	V Movement
● Fastball	68.8%	96.7 [113]	-7.7 [95]	-10.2 [118]
□ Sinker				
+ Cutter				
▲ Changeup	3.9%	89.2 [115]	-11.2 [100]	-22.9 [113]
× Splitter				
▽ Slider	27.3%	83.8 [97]	4.3 [98]	-41.3 [75]
◇ Curveball				
⊕ Slow Curveball				
✳ Knuckleball				
▼ Screwball				

New York Mets 2019

Jacob deGrom RHP

Born: 06/19/88 Age: 31 Bats: L Throws: R
Height: 6'4" Weight: 180 Origin: Round 9, 2010 Draft (#272 overall)

YEAR	TEAM	LVL	AGE	W	L	SV	G	GS	IP	H	HR	BB/9	K/9	K	GB%	BABIP
2016	NYN	MLB	28	7	8	0	24	24	148	142	15	2.2	8.7	143	47%	.312
2017	NYN	MLB	29	15	10	0	31	31	201¹	180	28	2.6	10.7	239	48%	.305
2018	NYN	MLB	30	10	9	0	32	32	217	152	10	1.9	11.2	269	48%	.281
2019	NYN	MLB	31	13	9	0	31	31	186	145	18	2.3	10.7	221	46%	.286

Breakout: 8% Improve: 29% Collapse: 28% Attrition: 6% MLB: 85%
Comparables: Erik Bedard, A.J. Burnett, CC Sabathia

I'm not sure how many superlatives are left to describe the reigning and defending National League Cy Young Award winner. deGrom's unbelievable 2018 season was the best in baseball over the past three years in terms of DRA-, and his 1.70 ERA underscored just how hard it was to mount an offense against his incredible right arm. In an era of Three True Outcomes, there's really only one that mattered against deGrom in 2018: the strikeout; the ace allowed just 10 dingers all season long despite throwing more innings than all but one pitcher. He was at his best against teams' best hitters and in the most pressure-packed situations. After years of being second fiddle behind Matt Harvey and Noah Syndergaard, the comparatively unassuming deGrom cut his long hair and got down to work. Now no Mets pitcher since Seaver can compare.

YEAR	TEAM	LVL	AGE	WHIP	ERA	DRA	WARP	MPH	FB%	WHF	CSP
2016	NYN	MLB	28	1.20	3.04	3.30	3.5	96.3	59.6	12.1	47.2
2017	NYN	MLB	29	1.19	3.53	3.02	5.7	97.2	55.5	14.5	49.5
2018	NYN	MLB	30	0.91	1.70	2.09	8.0	98.2	52.1	16.3	48.4
2019	NYN	MLB	31	1.02	2.91	3.23	3.9	96.6	54.5	14.8	48.2

Jacob deGrom, continued

Pitch Shape vs LHH

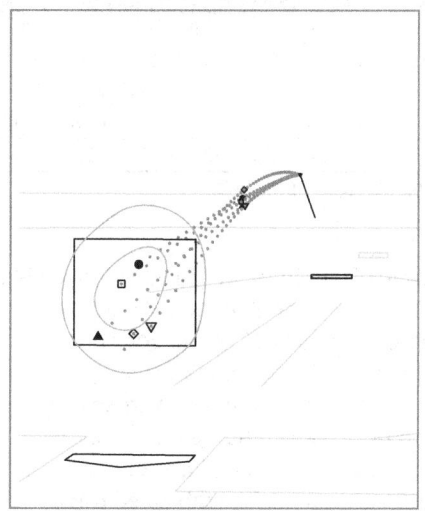

Pitch Shape vs RHH

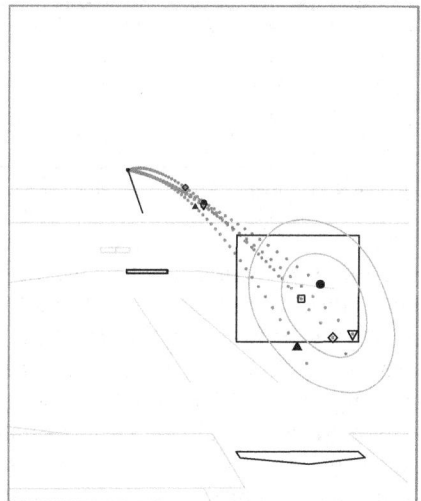

Type	Frequency	Velocity	H Movement	V Movement
● Fastball	42.6%	96.7 [113]	-3.6 [114]	-11.7 [113]
□ Sinker	9.5%	96.1 [118]	-10.4 [118]	-15.7 [115]
+ Cutter				
▲ Changeup	16.1%	89.6 [117]	-11.2 [100]	-25.6 [105]
× Splitter				
▽ Slider	23.9%	91.6 [132]	3.8 [95]	-23.9 [127]
◇ Curveball	7.9%	83.2 [118]	6.2 [93]	-38.7 [121]
⊕ Slow Curveball				
✷ Knuckleball				
▼ Screwball				

New York Mets 2019

Edwin Diaz RHP
Born: 03/22/94 Age: 25 Bats: R Throws: R
Height: 6'3" Weight: 165 Origin: Round 3, 2012 Draft (#98 overall)

YEAR	TEAM	LVL	AGE	W	L	SV	G	GS	IP	H	HR	BB/9	K/9	K	GB%	BABIP
2016	WTN	AA	22	3	3	1	16	6	40[2]	32	3	1.5	12.0	54	58%	.302
2016	SEA	MLB	22	0	4	18	49	0	51[2]	45	5	2.6	15.3	88	48%	.377
2017	SEA	MLB	23	4	6	34	66	0	66	44	10	4.4	12.1	89	41%	.236
2018	SEA	MLB	24	0	4	57	73	0	73[1]	41	5	2.1	15.2	124	47%	.281
2019	NYN	MLB	25	3	2	38	57	0	59	38	4	3.0	13.9	93	45%	.289

Breakout: 35%   Improve: 61%   Collapse: 18%   Attrition: 14%   MLB: 90%
Comparables: Jonathan Broxton, Francisco Liriano, Trevor Rosenthal

If you were ever curious what, say, the Battle of Carthage would have looked like if just one Carthaginian magically had a fully operational flamethrower, you could have just watched the way Diaz treated hitters in 2018 and gotten a rough idea. Less abstractly, if you gave a pitcher a fastball that could blister Satan's catching hand, a 90-mph slider capable of trans-dimensional movement and wondered what would happen if he halved his walk and home runs rates, well then here is the merchant of death/baseball closer for you. While relievers are arguably the game's most fickle alchemy, Diaz's raw stuff, established track record of dominance, and youth should combine to make him one of baseball's elite closers for years to come.

YEAR	TEAM	LVL	AGE	WHIP	ERA	DRA	WARP	MPH	FB%	WHF	CSP
2016	WTN	AA	22	0.96	2.21	1.72	1.6				
2016	SEA	MLB	22	1.16	2.79	1.84	1.9	101.0	67.5	20	51.1
2017	SEA	MLB	23	1.15	3.27	3.20	1.5	99.7	68.4	16.7	46
2018	SEA	MLB	24	0.79	1.96	1.77	2.7	99.3	62.4	20.7	48.4
2019	NYN	MLB	25	0.96	1.87	2.26	1.8	99.5	67.1	19.6	49.4

Edwin Diaz, continued

Pitch Shape vs LHH

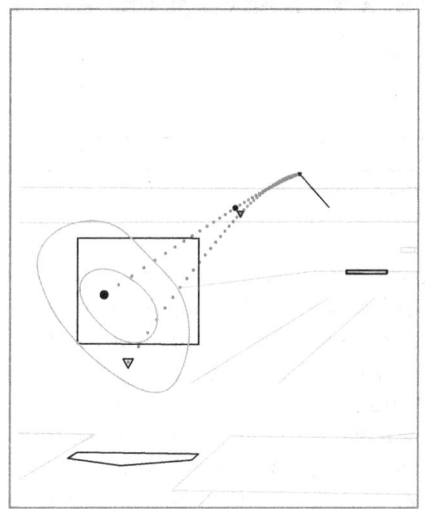

Pitch Shape vs RHH

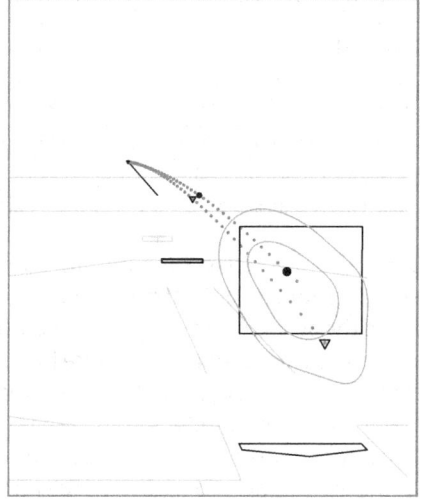

Type	Frequency	Velocity	H Movement	V Movement
● Fastball	62.4%	97.9 [117]	-9.1 [89]	-11.9 [112]
☐ Sinker				
+ Cutter				
▲ Changeup	0.3%	94.5 [136]	-12.7 [93]	-22.6 [114]
✕ Splitter				
▽ Slider	37.3%	89.7 [123]	2 [87]	-26.3 [120]
◇ Curveball				
⊕ Slow Curveball				
✳ Knuckleball				
▼ Screwball				

Jeurys Familia   RHP

Born: 10/10/89   Age: 29   Bats: R   Throws: R
Height: 6'3"   Weight: 240   Origin: International Free Agent, 2007

YEAR	TEAM	LVL	AGE	W	L	SV	G	GS	IP	H	HR	BB/9	K/9	K	GB%	BABIP
2016	NYN	MLB	26	3	4	51	78	0	77^2	63	1	3.6	9.7	84	66%	.304
2017	NYN	MLB	27	2	2	6	26	0	24^2	21	1	5.5	9.1	25	61%	.290
2018	NYN	MLB	28	4	4	17	40	0	40^2	36	1	3.1	9.5	43	52%	.315
2018	OAK	MLB	28	4	2	1	30	0	31^1	24	2	4.0	11.5	40	40%	.293
2019	NYN	MLB	29	3	2	3	52	0	54	45	6	4.0	10.1	61	52%	.289

Breakout: 26%   Improve: 45%   Collapse: 33%   Attrition: 16%   MLB: 98%
Comparables: Juan Rincon, Eric O'Flaherty, Peter Moylan

Oakland bolstered its bullpen with Familia two months before his free agency in exchange for a couple of non-impact minor leaguers, and he did his job both down the stretch — fitting into a deep and sometimes invincible relief corps — and in the Wild Card game, where he set down three straight Yankees in the eighth inning (though the A's were already trailing by five at that point). The major change in Familia's approach last year was pushing his slider usage from 15 percent of his pitches up to 28, largely at the expense of sinkers. As you would expect, his slider gets more whiffs and fewer grounders than his sinker; as you would expect, he pushed his strikeout rate over 10 per nine innings for the first time in his career, but also saw his ground-ball rate drop below 50 percent for the first time. DRA prefers his early work; then again, DRA lives in Bed-Stuy and has insufferable facial hair.

YEAR	TEAM	LVL	AGE	WHIP	ERA	DRA	WARP	MPH	FB%	WHF	CSP
2016	NYN	MLB	26	1.21	2.55	3.49	1.3	98.8	78	16	45.2
2017	NYN	MLB	27	1.46	4.38	6.48	-0.4	97.9	82.5	10.8	46.6
2018	NYN	MLB	28	1.23	2.88	4.62	0.1	97.8	70.2	12.6	49.6
2018	OAK	MLB	28	1.21	3.45	3.06	0.7	98.4	66.8	17.5	47.3
2019	NYN	MLB	29	1.27	3.61	4.06	0.5	97.6	73.7	14.6	47.1

Jeurys Familia, continued

Pitch Shape vs LHH

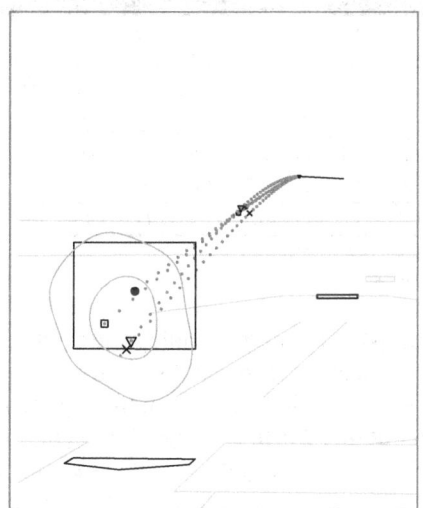

Pitch Shape vs RHH

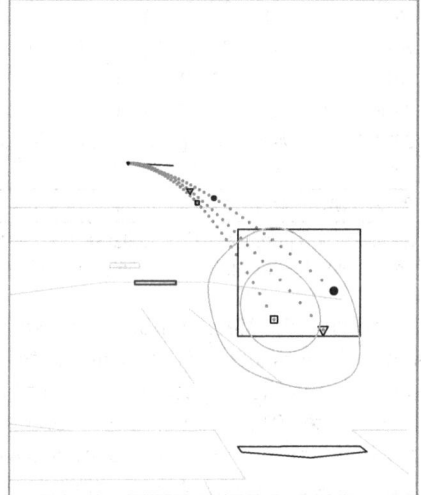

Type	Frequency	Velocity	H Movement	V Movement
● Fastball	16.5%	97 [114]	-8.8 [90]	-14.1 [105]
☐ Sinker	52.2%	96.6 [121]	-15.1 [79]	-21.4 [97]
+ Cutter				
▲ Changeup				
✕ Splitter	2.9%	92.2 [136]	-11.7 [87]	-25.4 [117]
▽ Slider	28.4%	88.4 [117]	1.5 [86]	-28.2 [114]
◇ Curveball				
⊕ Slow Curveball				
✳ Knuckleball				
▼ Screwball				

Mets Player Analysis - 69

Drew Gagnon RHP

Born: 06/26/90 Age: 29 Bats: R Throws: R
Height: 6'4" Weight: 215 Origin: Round 3, 2011 Draft (#100 overall)

YEAR	TEAM	LVL	AGE	W	L	SV	G	GS	IP	H	HR	BB/9	K/9	K	GB%	BABIP
2016	BLX	AA	26	1	0	1	5	1	13¹	4	0	2.7	10.1	15	43%	.143
2016	CSP	AAA	26	2	1	0	31	4	55	60	4	3.4	7.9	48	46%	.341
2017	SLC	AAA	27	1	1	0	31	10	86¹	95	6	4.1	8.7	83	40%	.355
2018	BIN	AA	28	1	0	0	1	1	6	2	0	1.5	7.5	5	62%	.125
2018	LVG	AAA	28	6	6	0	27	27	157²	151	23	2.5	9.5	167	50%	.314
2018	NYN	MLB	28	2	1	0	5	1	12	15	2	3.8	6.0	8	42%	.333
2019	NYN	MLB	29	1	1	0	15	0	16¹	13	2	3.5	9.3	17	44%	.289

Breakout: 7% Improve: 10% Collapse: 8% Attrition: 14% MLB: 26%
Comparables: Eddie Gamboa, Red Patterson, Robert Ray

Gagnon led the Mets' minor-league squads in games started, innings pitched and strikeouts last season, which earned him a mid-season spot start and a few late-season relief appearances—not to mention his first showing in these *Annual* pages since 2015. Even an improved strikeout rate doesn't change the ceiling we identified for him four years ago: he's likely either a pretty good Triple-A starter or a pretty bad big-league starter.

YEAR	TEAM	LVL	AGE	WHIP	ERA	DRA	WARP	MPH	FB%	WHF	CSP
2016	BLX	AA	26	0.60	0.00	3.45	0.2				
2016	CSP	AAA	26	1.47	5.56	4.07	0.6				
2017	SLC	AAA	27	1.55	6.25	3.60	1.8				
2018	BIN	AA	28	0.50	0.00	3.86	0.1				
2018	LVG	AAA	28	1.23	4.57	3.68	3.3				
2018	NYN	MLB	28	1.67	5.25	5.34	0.0	93.2	56.2	9	51.2
2019	NYN	MLB	29	1.21	3.58	4.04	0.1	92.5	56.2	9	51.2

Drew Gagnon, continued

Pitch Shape vs LHH

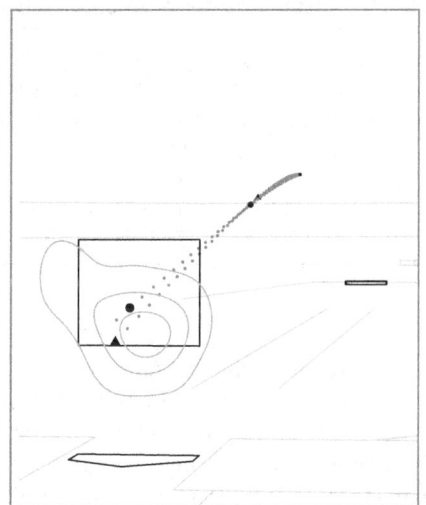

Pitch Shape vs RHH

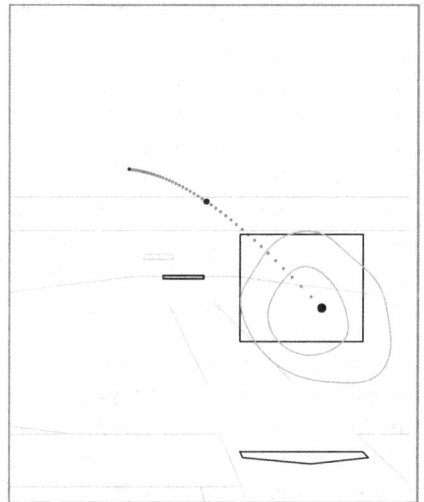

Type	Frequency	Velocity	H Movement	V Movement
● Fastball	56.2%	92 [98]	-11.7 [77]	-18.3 [92]
☐ Sinker				
+ Cutter				
▲ Changeup	25.2%	82.7 [89]	-13.9 [86]	-29.1 [95]
✕ Splitter				
▽ Slider	10.5%	85.3 [104]	1.5 [86]	-32.4 [102]
◇ Curveball	8.1%	77.8 [97]	10 [109]	-54 [87]
⊕ Slow Curveball				
✱ Knuckleball				
▼ Screwball				

Robert Gsellman RHP

Born: 07/18/93 Age: 25 Bats: R Throws: R
Height: 6'4" Weight: 205 Origin: Round 13, 2011 Draft (#402 overall)

YEAR	TEAM	LVL	AGE	W	L	SV	G	GS	IP	H	HR	BB/9	K/9	K	GB%	BABIP
2016	BIN	AA	22	3	4	0	11	11	66^1	57	2	2.0	6.5	48	57%	.282
2016	LVG	AAA	22	1	5	0	9	9	48^2	56	8	3.0	7.4	40	55%	.318
2016	NYN	MLB	22	4	2	0	8	7	44^2	42	1	3.0	8.5	42	57%	.325
2017	BIN	AA	23	1	0	0	4	4	12^1	15	0	3.6	6.6	9	76%	.366
2017	LVG	AAA	23	0	0	0	1	1	6	10	1	4.5	4.5	3	50%	.391
2017	NYN	MLB	23	8	7	0	25	22	119^2	138	17	3.2	6.2	82	51%	.303
2018	NYN	MLB	24	6	3	13	68	0	80	76	8	3.2	7.9	70	52%	.291
2019	NYN	MLB	25	3	3	2	57	0	59	53	5	3.3	8.8	58	50%	.287

Breakout: 18% Improve: 50% Collapse: 20% Attrition: 26% MLB: 95%
Comparables: Kyle Freeland, Martin Perez, Chad Kuhl

Noah Syndergaard's wingman went through a season of change. After converting to the 'pen full-time this year, Gsellman's year had more phases than Kitty Pryde. For the first month, he was a nightmare for opposing teams, a multi-inning relief ace capable of striking out the side or ripping through two or three innings. By the midpoint of May, he'd already thrown more than 26 innings and, perhaps starting to wear down a little, looked like a fairly average middle reliever. Finally, at the end of the year, he did a respectable impression of a one-and-done, second-division closer after incumbent Jeurys Familia was dealt away. Another year working out of the bullpen might see him gain a little more comfort, and hopefully see his velocity tick back up to the 2016 breakout levels, but the ceiling today isn't anything like the "7/6" that catapulted his profile years ago.

YEAR	TEAM	LVL	AGE	WHIP	ERA	DRA	WARP	MPH	FB%	WHF	CSP
2016	BIN	AA	22	1.09	2.71	3.63	1.2				
2016	LVG	AAA	22	1.48	5.73	7.75	-1.3				
2016	NYN	MLB	22	1.28	2.42	4.24	0.6	96.1	63.5	10.6	47.6
2017	BIN	AA	23	1.62	2.92	4.64	0.1				
2017	LVG	AAA	23	2.17	7.50	3.62	0.1				
2017	NYN	MLB	23	1.50	5.19	5.77	-0.3	94.7	63.4	8.1	45.7
2018	NYN	MLB	24	1.30	4.28	4.38	0.5	96.1	62.8	10.8	49.3
2019	NYN	MLB	25	1.23	3.54	4.00	0.6	95.2	64.7	9.7	48.8

Robert Gsellman, continued

Pitch Shape vs LHH

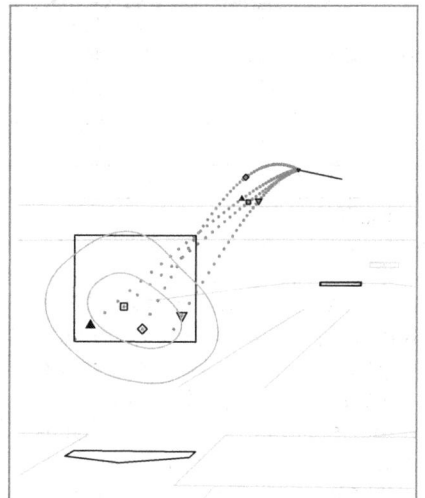

Pitch Shape vs RHH

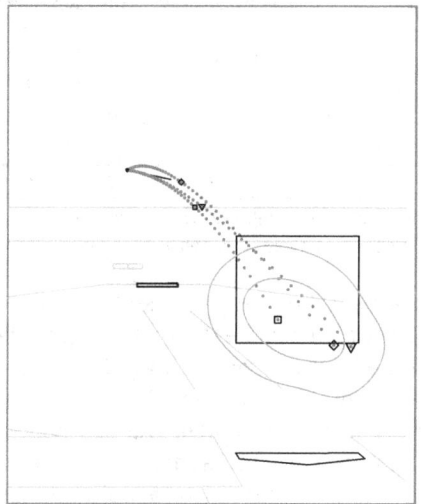

Type	Frequency	Velocity	H Movement	V Movement
● Fastball	2.7%	94.6 [107]	-10.5 [82]	-15.2 [102]
☐ Sinker	60.2%	94.5 [110]	-14.7 [82]	-18.8 [105]
+ Cutter				
▲ Changeup	8.7%	87.2 [107]	-13.4 [89]	-25 [107]
✕ Splitter				
▽ Slider	16.5%	90.2 [126]	-0.2 [78]	-24.5 [125]
◇ Curveball	11.9%	82.3 [114]	7.8 [100]	-44.8 [107]
⊕ Slow Curveball				
✳ Knuckleball				
▼ Screwball				

Seth Lugo   RHP

Born: 11/17/89   Age: 29   Bats: R   Throws: R
Height: 6'4"   Weight: 225   Origin: Round 34, 2011 Draft (#1032 overall)

YEAR	TEAM	LVL	AGE	W	L	SV	G	GS	IP	H	HR	BB/9	K/9	K	GB%	BABIP
2016	LVG	AAA	26	3	4	0	21	14	73^1	103	10	2.5	7.6	62	46%	.375
2016	NYN	MLB	26	5	2	0	17	8	64	49	7	3.0	6.3	45	46%	.230
2017	BIN	AA	27	1	1	0	2	2	13	14	1	1.4	10.4	15	54%	.382
2017	NYN	MLB	27	7	5	0	19	18	101^1	114	13	2.2	7.5	85	43%	.325
2018	NYN	MLB	28	3	4	3	54	5	101^1	81	9	2.5	9.1	103	47%	.269
2019	NYN	MLB	29	5	4	0	63	6	89	81	10	2.9	9.0	90	45%	.291

Breakout: 32%   Improve: 52%   Collapse: 17%   Attrition: 18%   MLB: 79%
Comparables: Craig Stammen, Brandon Workman, Chris Narveson

The Mets' best relief pitcher last season was a guy who would've started for many teams in the National League. The King of Spin Rate took to the bullpen like a fish to water and logged over 78 innings in relief while also popping up for five spot starts. In relief, the durability issues that have dogged him faded into the background, and his velocity spiked in shorter stints. Best of all, his well-regarded curveball added extra movement and stayed a premier out-pitch, allowing him to work as a multi-inning, multi-pitch Swiss Army knife for the Amazins. His underlying peripherals don't exactly reflect how good he's been at limiting runs, but he remains a solid example of the modern multi-faceted bullpen weapon every team needs.

YEAR	TEAM	LVL	AGE	WHIP	ERA	DRA	WARP	MPH	FB%	WHF	CSP
2016	LVG	AAA	26	1.68	6.50	4.89	0.3				
2016	NYN	MLB	26	1.09	2.67	4.62	0.5	95.9	57.5	10.2	49
2017	BIN	AA	27	1.23	2.77	2.81	0.4				
2017	NYN	MLB	27	1.37	4.71	5.26	0.3	93.8	56.8	9.7	50.3
2018	NYN	MLB	28	1.08	2.66	3.82	1.4	96.6	48.8	10.8	50
2019	NYN	MLB	29	1.23	3.74	4.17	0.7	94.8	53.2	10.3	49.8

Seth Lugo, continued

Pitch Shape vs LHH   **Pitch Shape vs RHH**

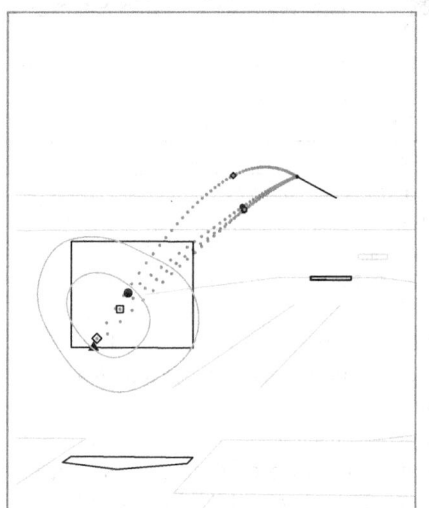 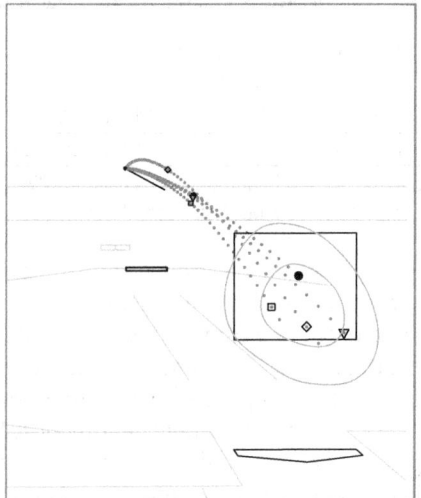

Type	Frequency	Velocity	H Movement	V Movement
● Fastball	25.6%	94.8 [107]	-6.5 [101]	-13 [109]
□ Sinker	23.2%	93.8 [106]	-13.7 [91]	-17.6 [109]
+ Cutter				
▲ Changeup	7.6%	87.7 [109]	-13.5 [88]	-23.7 [111]
× Splitter				
▽ Slider	11.7%	88.3 [117]	3.3 [93]	-25.8 [121]
◇ Curveball	31.9%	80.3 [107]	11 [113]	-51.1 [93]
⊕ Slow Curveball				
✳ Knuckleball				
▼ Screwball				

Steven Matz LHP

Born: 05/29/91 Age: 28 Bats: R Throws: L
Height: 6'2" Weight: 200 Origin: Round 2, 2009 Draft (#72 overall)

YEAR	TEAM	LVL	AGE	W	L	SV	G	GS	IP	H	HR	BB/9	K/9	K	GB%	BABIP
2016	NYN	MLB	25	9	8	0	22	22	132^1	129	14	2.1	8.8	129	54%	.312
2017	LVG	AAA	26	0	1	0	3	3	13^1	13	3	1.4	11.5	17	35%	.323
2017	NYN	MLB	26	2	7	0	13	13	66^2	83	12	2.6	6.5	48	49%	.329
2018	NYN	MLB	27	5	11	0	30	30	154	134	25	3.4	8.9	152	50%	.267
2019	NYN	MLB	28	9	8	0	26	26	130	113	13	2.7	9.2	133	49%	.289

Breakout: 22%   Improve: 57%   Collapse: 10%   Attrition: 14%   MLB: 91%
Comparables: Zach McAllister, John Maine, Wade Miley

He did it. Against all odds, Matz improbably made 30 starts in a Mets uniform, something few imagined given his perennial injury concerns. Given how dynamic this southpaw had previously been during his limited periods of health, did this lead him to a long-awaited, media-frenzied breakout? Nah. Not only was he eclipsed by his talented rotation-mates, he never seemed dominant or, for that matter, totally healthy in 2018. He managed only about five innings per outing over all of those starts, and that left the unpredictable Mets bullpen in play to ruin those games he did appear in. There were still MRIs and a brief DL stint that made everyone think he was about to fall apart, but in August and September the New York native churned out the best starts of his season, including a seven-inning, 11-strikeout performance you can dream on. Even after an improbable full season as a starter, Matz remains as risky and as tantalizing as ever.

YEAR	TEAM	LVL	AGE	WHIP	ERA	DRA	WARP	MPH	FB%	WHF	CSP
2016	NYN	MLB	25	1.21	3.40	3.34	3.1	96.0	61.5	10.4	50.4
2017	LVG	AAA	26	1.12	6.75	3.98	0.3				
2017	NYN	MLB	26	1.53	6.07	6.03	-0.3	94.5	59.1	7.9	48.4
2018	NYN	MLB	27	1.25	3.97	3.62	3.0	95.0	60	10	52.6
2019	NYN	MLB	28	1.16	3.50	3.89	1.8	94.6	60.6	9.8	51

Steven Matz, continued

Pitch Shape vs LHH

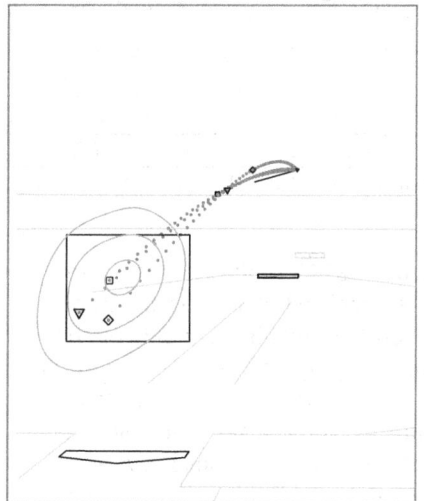

Pitch Shape vs RHH

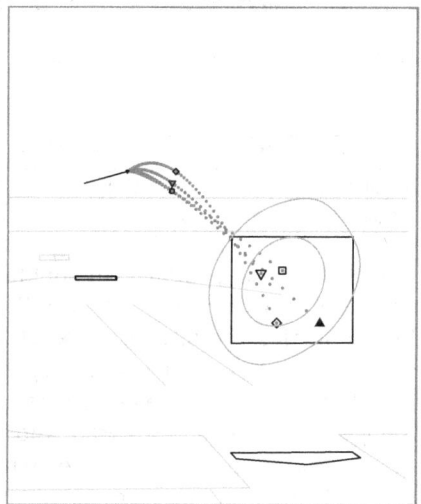

Type	Frequency	Velocity	H Movement	V Movement
● Fastball				
☐ Sinker	60.0%	94 [107]	13.8 [90]	-18 [108]
+ Cutter				
▲ Changeup	15.9%	84.7 [98]	15.3 [78]	-29.3 [94]
✕ Splitter				
▽ Slider	8.4%	88.8 [119]	0.9 [75]	-26.6 [119]
◇ Curveball	15.7%	79.1 [102]	-8.5 [103]	-48 [100]
⊕ Slow Curveball				
✳ Knuckleball				
▼ Screwball				

New York Mets 2019

Corey Oswalt RHP
Born: 09/03/93 Age: 25 Bats: R Throws: R
Height: 6'5" Weight: 250 Origin: Round 7, 2012 Draft (#230 overall)

YEAR	TEAM	LVL	AGE	W	L	SV	G	GS	IP	H	HR	BB/9	K/9	K	GB%	BABIP
2016	SLU	A+	22	4	2	0	14	13	67²	73	4	2.4	9.0	68	60%	.348
2017	BIN	AA	23	12	5	0	24	24	134¹	118	9	2.7	8.0	119	49%	.290
2018	LVG	AAA	24	4	4	0	11	11	52¹	58	9	3.4	8.9	52	45%	.331
2018	NYN	MLB	24	3	3	0	17	12	64²	69	14	2.8	6.3	45	43%	.276
2019	NYN	MLB	25	2	3	0	8	8	40	39	5	2.9	8.1	36	46%	.293

Breakout: 9%   Improve: 38%   Collapse: 20%   Attrition: 40%   MLB: 75%
Comparables: Jarlin Garcia, Luis Cessa, Dillon Peters

Despite very strong numbers in Double-A during 2017, this big right-hander was never really classified as a prospect. Oswalt's lack of helium was mostly due to the fact that his fastball lives in the (very) low 90s and his secondary pitches barely flash average. While that can get you far grinding it out in Binghamton, it's just not the profile of a regular starter in today's MLB. At his best, Oswalt's calling is as an emergency starter who can keep you in a game but will have trouble racking up whiffs. Every team needs one or two of those guys at the ready in Triple-A, but no team can afford to give him another 12 starts in a season.

YEAR	TEAM	LVL	AGE	WHIP	ERA	DRA	WARP	MPH	FB%	WHF	CSP
2016	SLU	A+	22	1.34	4.12	3.35	1.6				
2017	BIN	AA	23	1.18	2.28	3.47	2.7				
2018	LVG	AAA	24	1.49	6.02	6.34	-0.5				
2018	NYN	MLB	24	1.38	5.85	5.73	-0.4	92.5	67	8	47.8
2019	NYN	MLB	25	1.29	4.25	4.71	0.2	92.2	68.6	8.2	49

Corey Oswalt, continued

Pitch Shape vs LHH

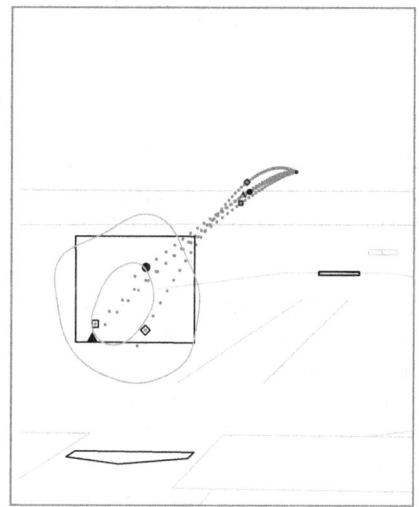

Pitch Shape vs RHH

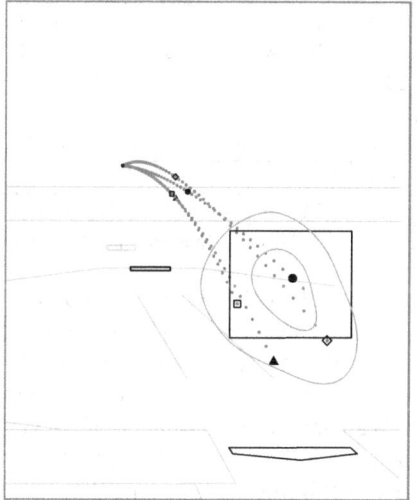

Type	Frequency	Velocity	H Movement	V Movement
● Fastball	46.7%	91.2 [96]	-7 [98]	-15.4 [101]
☐ Sinker	20.3%	90.3 [89]	-12.9 [97]	-20.4 [100]
+ Cutter	0.4%	86.9 [89]	-1.1 [82]	-22.9 [103]
▲ Changeup	14.9%	84.2 [95]	-10 [107]	-30.1 [92]
✕ Splitter				
▽ Slider				
◇ Curveball	17.7%	81 [109]	5.5 [90]	-43.2 [111]
✤ Slow Curveball				
✻ Knuckleball				
▼ Screwball				

Hector Santiago LHP

Born: 12/16/87   Age: 31   Bats: R   Throws: L
Height: 6'0"   Weight: 215   Origin: Round 30, 2006 Draft (#915 overall)

YEAR	TEAM	LVL	AGE	W	L	SV	G	GS	IP	H	HR	BB/9	K/9	K	GB%	BABIP
2016	ANA	MLB	28	10	4	0	22	22	120^2	104	20	4.3	8.0	107	40%	.257
2016	MIN	MLB	28	3	6	0	11	11	61^1	65	13	3.2	5.4	37	28%	.264
2017	MIN	MLB	29	4	8	0	15	14	70^1	70	15	4.0	6.5	51	32%	.263
2017	ROC	AAA	29	1	2	0	7	7	23^2	21	4	6.5	9.5	25	27%	.270
2018	CHA	MLB	30	6	3	2	49	7	102	101	16	5.3	9.1	103	35%	.308
2019	NYN	MLB	31	1	1	0	21	0	21	19	3	4.4	9.0	22	35%	.280

Breakout: 20%   Improve: 56%   Collapse: 12%   Attrition: 13%   MLB: 88%
Comparables: J.A. Happ, Todd Wellemeyer, Vicente Padilla

It's fairly likely that Hector Santiago knows it's a little rough to watch him pitch. He knows his four-seam fastball moves a lot and moves strangely. Algorithms often mark it as a two-seamer (it isn't, he insists) but computer models' struggles to explain its movement mirrors the struggles of its handler. He knows he's always going to walk plenty of guys, he knows he's not going to generate easy ground ball outs with it, and he knows in turn that he will always allow plenty of home runs. But the thing moves, it's given life to a career that never was supposed to last this long, and it has allowed him to miss bats even as his velocity has declined. Back and shoulder problems made Santiago settle for a minor-league deal coming into 2018, and wildness plagued him as he pitched his way out of the Sox starting rotation, but he just kept throwing and trusting that darting four-seamer, through all the snags and scrapes, and he'll probably find his way to another major league job—however unglamorous—because of it.

YEAR	TEAM	LVL	AGE	WHIP	ERA	DRA	WARP	MPH	FB%	WHF	CSP
2016	ANA	MLB	28	1.33	4.25	5.51	-0.2	95.3	60.7	9.9	49.3
2016	MIN	MLB	28	1.42	5.58	7.77	-1.7	93.8	60.7	7.7	48.7
2017	MIN	MLB	29	1.44	5.63	7.41	-1.4	93.0	60.4	8.1	48.4
2017	ROC	AAA	29	1.61	5.32	4.20	0.4				
2018	CHA	MLB	30	1.58	4.41	6.73	-2.0	93.0	68	9.4	49.3
2019	NYN	MLB	31	1.32	4.89	5.09	-0.1	92.9	63.2	9	48.6

Hector Santiago, continued

Pitch Shape vs LHH

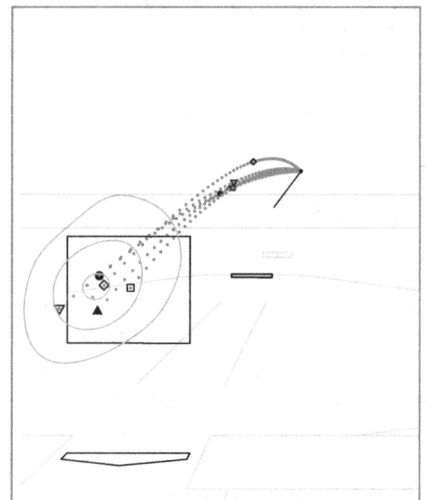

Pitch Shape vs RHH

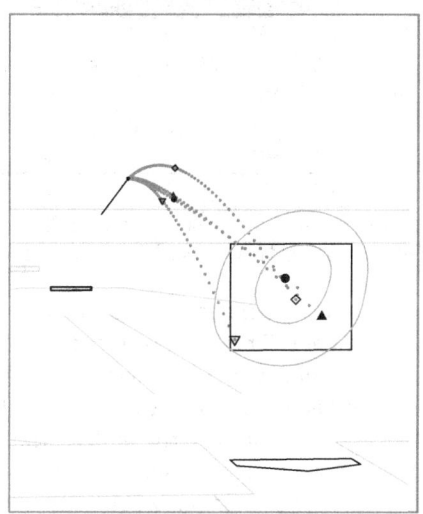

Type	Frequency	Velocity	H Movement	V Movement
● Fastball	65.8%	91.2 [96]	11.1 [79]	-16.5 [98]
☐ Sinker	2.1%	88.7 [81]	14.4 [85]	-22.7 [92]
+ Cutter				
▲ Changeup	20.6%	82.5 [89]	13.8 [87]	-27 [101]
✕ Splitter				
▽ Slider	4.0%	83.5 [96]	-3.2 [93]	-31 [106]
◇ Curveball	7.2%	74.8 [87]	-5.8 [91]	-48.6 [99]
⊕ Slow Curveball				
✴ Knuckleball				
▼ Screwball	0.3%	76.2	15.4	-35.7

Paul Sewald   RHP

Born: 05/26/90   Age: 29   Bats: R   Throws: R
Height: 6'3"   Weight: 207   Origin: Round 10, 2012 Draft (#320 overall)

YEAR	TEAM	LVL	AGE	W	L	SV	G	GS	IP	H	HR	BB/9	K/9	K	GB%	BABIP
2016	LVG	AAA	26	5	3	19	56	0	65²	58	9	2.9	11.0	80	38%	.295
2017	LVG	AAA	27	1	0	4	8	0	8²	7	1	2.1	12.5	12	27%	.286
2017	NYN	MLB	27	0	6	0	57	0	65¹	58	8	2.9	9.5	69	35%	.287
2018	LVG	AAA	28	3	0	1	7	0	8	7	0	1.1	7.9	7	62%	.292
2018	NYN	MLB	28	0	7	2	46	0	56¹	62	8	3.7	9.3	58	32%	.331
2019	NYN	MLB	29	2	2	0	36	0	38	36	6	3.6	9.0	38	37%	.290

Breakout: 17%   Improve: 40%   Collapse: 22%   Attrition: 24%   MLB: 76%
Comparables: Brad Brach, Josh Osich, Josh Fields

Sewald the slider specialist is a unique convocation of a few extremely *Metsy* throughlines. First, he was once the poster boy for ridiculously low minor league salaries while working for a team owned by notorious spendthrifts. This year, he was worked exceptionally hard out of the bullpen during an excellent April and May, which left little in the tank for the rest of the season. (This is something new manager Mickey Callaway apparently learned from departing manager and expert relief-burner Terry Collins.) Now, after giving away more hits than the Neptunes at the end of 2018, Sewald is now 0-13 in two (almost) full big-league seasons despite projecting as an average middle reliever going forward. If that doesn't make him a lovable loser–and therefore a Met in the truest sense–I don't know what does.

YEAR	TEAM	LVL	AGE	WHIP	ERA	DRA	WARP	MPH	FB%	WHF	CSP
2016	LVG	AAA	26	1.20	3.29	3.69	1.0				
2017	LVG	AAA	27	1.04	2.08	2.02	0.3				
2017	NYN	MLB	27	1.21	4.55	3.59	1.2	93.2	64	12.3	50.4
2018	LVG	AAA	28	1.00	1.12	6.68	-0.1				
2018	NYN	MLB	28	1.51	6.07	4.24	0.4	92.4	63.4	10.3	50.6
2019	NYN	MLB	29	1.35	4.93	5.13	-0.1	92.1	63.6	11.2	50.5

Paul Sewald, continued

Pitch Shape vs LHH

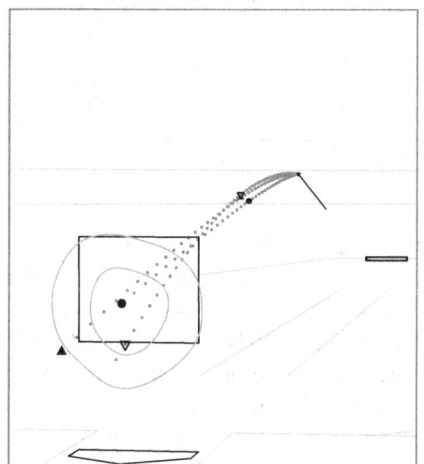

Pitch Shape vs RHH

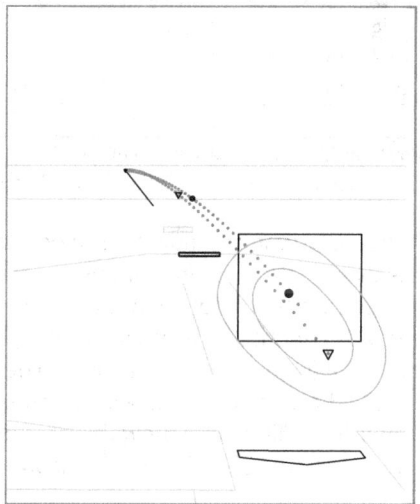

Type	Frequency	Velocity	H Movement	V Movement
● Fastball	59.2%	91 [95]	-10.6 [82]	-17.7 [94]
☐ Sinker	4.2%	90.2 [89]	-15.3 [78]	-27.7 [76]
+ Cutter				
▲ Changeup	6.3%	83.9 [94]	-12.8 [92]	-30.4 [91]
✕ Splitter				
▽ Slider	30.3%	81.9 [88]	7.6 [112]	-33.8 [98]
◇ Curveball				
⊕ Slow Curveball				
✱ Knuckleball				
▼ Screwball				

Noah Syndergaard RHP
Born: 08/29/92   Age: 26   Bats: L   Throws: R
Height: 6'6"   Weight: 240   Origin: Round 1, 2010 Draft (#38 overall)

YEAR	TEAM	LVL	AGE	W	L	SV	G	GS	IP	H	HR	BB/9	K/9	K	GB%	BABIP
2016	NYN	MLB	23	14	9	0	31	30	183^2	168	11	2.1	10.7	218	52%	.334
2017	NYN	MLB	24	1	2	0	7	7	30^1	29	0	0.9	10.1	34	59%	.337
2018	NYN	MLB	25	13	4	0	25	25	154^1	148	9	2.3	9.0	155	50%	.320
2019	NYN	MLB	26	11	8	0	28	28	168	146	15	2.5	10.0	187	50%	.299

Breakout: 22%   Improve: 63%   Collapse: 17%   Attrition: 7%   MLB: 96%
Comparables: Alex Wood, Jaime Garcia, Matt Garza

Any season where Syndergaard doesn't strike out 15 hitters per game and win the Cy Young Award unanimously gets considered a disappointment. No, that's not fair, but that's how things tend to work when you're built like a Norse god, throw harder than any other starting pitcher, and play in New York. He pitched around a finger injury and a disease he picked up at a summer camp, but was mostly the same old Thor, a slight drop in his velocity and strikeout rate notwithstanding. Somehow this perturbed his team's front office enough to consider trading him in the offseason.

On a rate basis, Noah Syndergaard was the sixth-best starting pitcher in baseball last season, just behind AL Cy Young winner Blake Snell. In a "down year," Thor thrived on the strength of his velocity (yes it's still elite), his tenacity and a slider that can only be accurately described using swear words. If you want to consider his 2018 a disappointment, go ahead, but it's only because he's a run of good health and pinch of luck away from putting up the world-beating season everyone seems to be waiting for.

YEAR	TEAM	LVL	AGE	WHIP	ERA	DRA	WARP	MPH	FB%	WHF	CSP
2016	NYN	MLB	23	1.15	2.60	2.28	6.5	100.5	59.1	15.3	47.5
2017	NYN	MLB	24	1.05	2.97	2.54	1.0	100.0	51.3	14.9	47
2018	NYN	MLB	25	1.21	3.03	2.47	5.0	99.3	53.7	14.4	47.5
2019	NYN	MLB	26	1.15	3.08	3.42	3.2	99.4	56.6	15	48.2

Noah Syndergaard, continued

Pitch Shape vs LHH

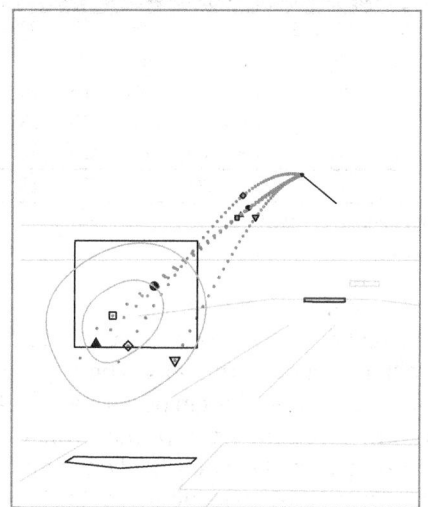

Pitch Shape vs RHH

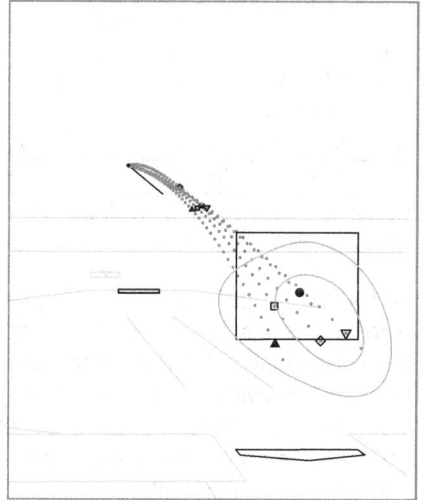

Type	Frequency	Velocity	H Movement	V Movement
● Fastball	20.7%	98.1 [118]	-5.7 [105]	-12.1 [112]
□ Sinker	33.0%	98 [127]	-12.1 [104]	-15.1 [117]
+ Cutter				
▲ Changeup	15.7%	90.9 [122]	-13.1 [90]	-21.8 [116]
× Splitter				
▽ Slider	20.9%	92.6 [136]	2.7 [91]	-22.4 [131]
◇ Curveball	9.8%	83.6 [119]	7.9 [100]	-35.4 [128]
⊕ Slow Curveball				
✳ Knuckleball				
▼ Screwball				

New York Mets 2019

Jason Vargas LHP
Born: 02/02/83 Age: 36 Bats: L Throws: L
Height: 6'0" Weight: 215 Origin: Round 2, 2004 Draft (#68 overall)

YEAR	TEAM	LVL	AGE	W	L	SV	G	GS	IP	H	HR	BB/9	K/9	K	GB%	BABIP
2016	OMA	AAA	33	0	2	0	3	3	13²	16	3	0.7	11.9	18	35%	.382
2016	KCA	MLB	33	0	0	0	3	3	12	8	1	2.2	8.2	11	36%	.219
2017	KCA	MLB	34	18	11	0	32	32	179²	181	27	2.9	6.7	134	41%	.289
2018	BRO	A-	35	0	0	0	2	2	12	7	2	0.0	14.2	19	30%	.238
2018	NYN	MLB	35	7	9	0	20	20	92	100	18	2.9	8.2	84	42%	.307
2019	NYN	MLB	36	8	8	0	23	23	121	112	17	2.9	8.9	120	41%	.288

Breakout: 18% Improve: 36% Collapse: 16% Attrition: 13% MLB: 72%
Comparables: Kenshin Kawakami, Kyle Lohse, Roy Oswalt

You shouldn't sign Vargas expecting 18 wins, or even above-average performance; leading the AL in wins before signing his two-year deal with the Mets was a trick of the light, nothing more than a mirage. This lefty is best acquired to provide innings and the veneer of stability—if not in performance, at least in showing up on the regular. Every team needs innings, especially when you're the Mets, but 2018 started rough for Vargas and he barely held on to his rotation spot long enough to turn it around over the last two months of the season. The Mets will hope that his 3.60 ERA and a strikeout per inning over his last 10 starts was a glimmer of hope for 2019 and not a dead-cat bounce for a pitcher who may be viable only as a reliever at this phase of his career.

YEAR	TEAM	LVL	AGE	WHIP	ERA	DRA	WARP	MPH	FB%	WHF	CSP
2016	OMA	AAA	33	1.24	5.93	2.55	0.4				
2016	KCA	MLB	33	0.92	2.25	5.58	0.0	89.0	52.2	10.5	40.4
2017	KCA	MLB	34	1.33	4.16	4.48	2.2	87.5	46.8	10.2	45
2018	BRO	A-	35	0.58	1.50	2.40	0.4				
2018	NYN	MLB	35	1.41	5.77	4.11	1.3	88.2	54.4	11.7	47.3
2019	NYN	MLB	36	1.23	4.11	4.56	0.7	86.6	48.8	10.5	43.9

Jason Vargas, continued

Pitch Shape vs LHH   **Pitch Shape vs RHH**

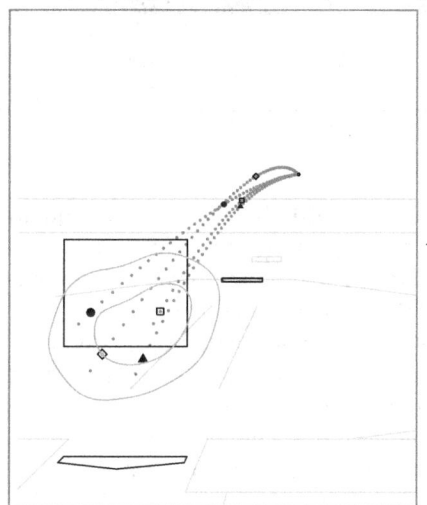 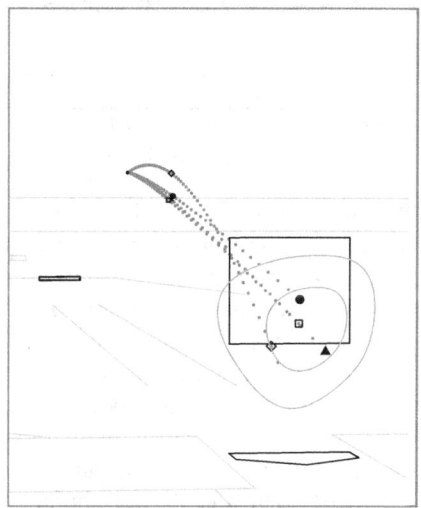

Type	Frequency	Velocity	H Movement	V Movement
● Fastball	18.1%	87 [82]	9 [89]	-17.5 [95]
☐ Sinker	36.3%	86.8 [72]	13.7 [91]	-21.5 [96]
+ Cutter				
▲ Changeup	29.5%	81.1 [83]	15 [80]	-27.4 [100]
✕ Splitter				
▽ Slider				
◇ Curveball	16.2%	74 [83]	-8.7 [104]	-53.1 [89]
✥ Slow Curveball				
✳ Knuckleball				
▼ Screwball				

Zack Wheeler   RHP
Born: 05/30/90   Age: 29   Bats: L   Throws: R
Height: 6'4"   Weight: 195   Origin: Round 1, 2009 Draft (#6 overall)

YEAR	TEAM	LVL	AGE	W	L	SV	G	GS	IP	H	HR	BB/9	K/9	K	GB%	BABIP
2017	NYN	MLB	27	3	7	0	17	17	86^1	97	15	4.2	8.4	81	48%	.332
2018	NYN	MLB	28	12	7	0	29	29	182^1	150	14	2.7	8.8	179	46%	.279
2019	NYN	MLB	29	10	9	0	28	28	159	143	20	3.2	9.1	162	44%	.289

Breakout: 16%   Improve: 38%   Collapse: 23%   Attrition: 10%   MLB: 96%
Comparables: Matt Garza, Andy Messersmith, John Lackey

Three long years separated Wheeler's impressive 2014 breakout and his equally stellar 2018. Between those bookends, the righty lost two full seasons to Tommy John surgery and its complications, then added an up-and-down 2017 marred by further injury and inconsistency. Until this year, his stock was in freefall—after all, what good is a hurler who can't stay healthy? Would all that time off hamper his already questionable command? It didn't appear so, as he finally harnessed his off-speed stuff, walked fewer batters than ever and grew into a full-on no. 2 starter. Usually it's the year before free agency where a pitcher really makes their money, but Wheeler has flashed enough top-end potential that all he needs to do is finish 2019 upright for him to get a very impressive payday when he hits free agency in nine months.

YEAR	TEAM	LVL	AGE	WHIP	ERA	DRA	WARP	MPH	FB%	WHF	CSP
2017	NYN	MLB	27	1.59	5.21	5.30	0.3	96.6	61.7	10	49.5
2018	NYN	MLB	28	1.12	3.31	3.01	4.8	98.3	58.3	12	48.2
2019	NYN	MLB	29	1.25	3.98	4.40	1.2	97.1	59.3	11.4	48.8

Zack Wheeler, continued

Pitch Shape vs LHH	Pitch Shape vs RHH
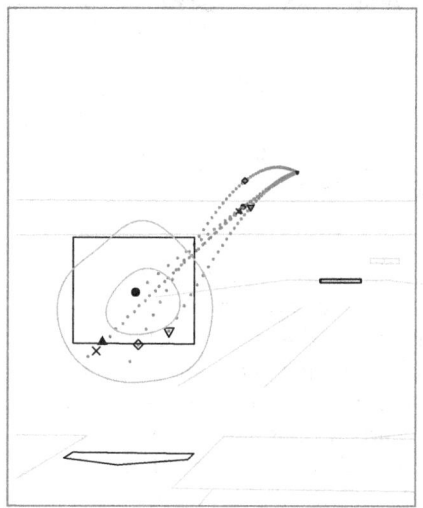	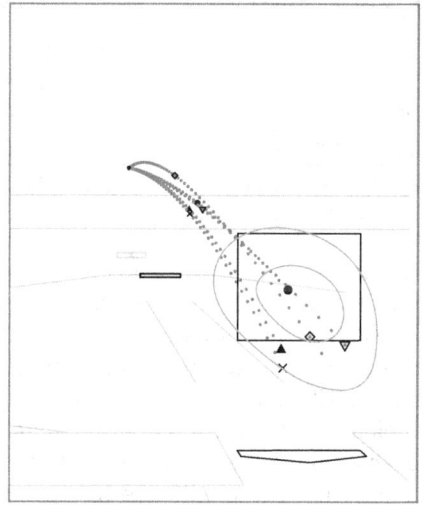

Type	Frequency	Velocity	H Movement	V Movement
● Fastball	58.3%	96.5 [113]	-9.2 [89]	-12.4 [111]
☐ Sinker				
+ Cutter				
▲ Changeup	6.2%	89.3 [116]	-10.5 [104]	-21.3 [118]
✕ Splitter	5.9%	89.8 [123]	-10.8 [90]	-23.5 [126]
▽ Slider	19.2%	91.5 [131]	1.9 [87]	-23 [130]
◇ Curveball	10.5%	79.8 [105]	7.5 [99]	-48.2 [100]
✥ Slow Curveball				
✳ Knuckleball				
▼ Screwball				

Justin Wilson LHP

Born: 08/18/87 Age: 31 Bats: L Throws: L
Height: 6'2" Weight: 205 Origin: Round 5, 2008 Draft (#144 overall)

YEAR	TEAM	LVL	AGE	W	L	SV	G	GS	IP	H	HR	BB/9	K/9	K	GB%	BABIP
2016	DET	MLB	28	4	5	1	66	0	58^2	61	6	2.6	10.0	65	56%	.340
2017	DET	MLB	29	3	4	13	42	0	40^1	22	5	3.6	12.3	55	38%	.210
2017	CHN	MLB	29	1	0	0	23	0	17^2	18	0	9.7	12.7	25	37%	.391
2018	CHN	MLB	30	4	5	0	71	0	54^2	45	5	5.4	11.4	69	37%	.310
2019	NYN	MLB	31	3	2	0	46	0	49	41	6	4.2	10.7	58	43%	.293

Breakout: 38% Improve: 47% Collapse: 32% Attrition: 18% MLB: 96%
Comparables: Francisco Rodriguez, Steve Cishek, Joel Hanrahan

For some reason, Wilson and the Cubs have been about as good a combination as a Chicago hot dog and ketchup. His spell as one of the game's most devastating closers lasted only a few months with the Tigers, just long enough to convince the Cubs they were getting an elite bullpen arm. Any semblance of control fell off the back of the truck on I-94, even if the ERA might fool us into thinking 2018 was just fine. If this were a heartwarming sports movie, the lovable clubhouse attendant would have turned up at just the right time—just before Wilson entered Game 163 against the Brewers, for example—brandishing Wilson's magic glove, the source of all his control. Instead Orlando Arcia singled off a misplaced Wilson slider to start the game-winning rally and the Cubs were, once again, left wondering what happened to the guy they traded for.

YEAR	TEAM	LVL	AGE	WHIP	ERA	DRA	WARP	MPH	FB%	WHF	CSP
2016	DET	MLB	28	1.33	4.14	4.15	0.6	97.7	65.1	13.7	46.3
2017	DET	MLB	29	0.94	2.68	3.24	0.9	97.1	64.3	16	49.2
2017	CHN	MLB	29	2.09	5.09	6.03	-0.2	97.0	64.3	9.2	46.5
2018	CHN	MLB	30	1.43	3.46	4.65	0.2	96.0	75.4	13.4	51.9
2019	NYN	MLB	31	1.30	3.79	4.21	0.3	95.9	68.6	13.4	48.9

Justin Wilson, continued

Pitch Shape vs LHH

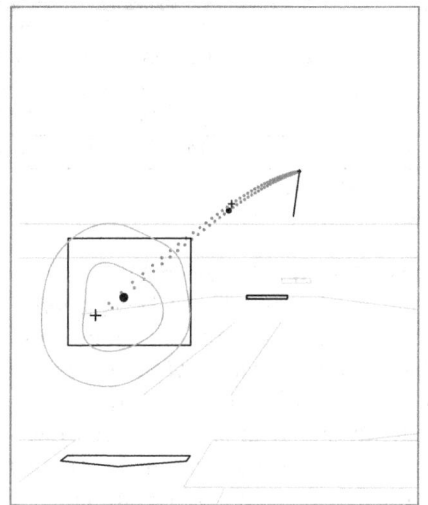

Pitch Shape vs RHH

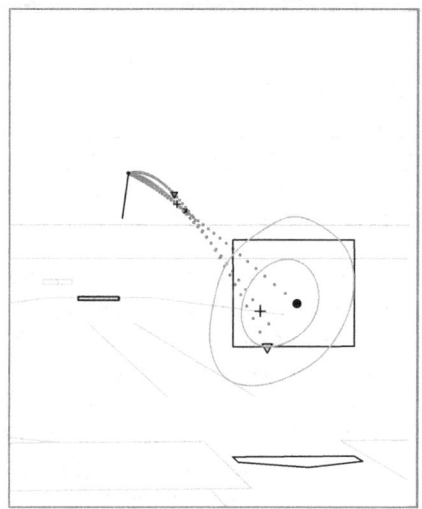

Type	Frequency	Velocity	H Movement	V Movement
● Fastball	75.4%	95.1 [108]	4.1 [112]	-10.5 [117]
☐ Sinker				
+ Cutter	15.2%	91.4 [116]	-3.2 [108]	-19.6 [116]
▲ Changeup				
✕ Splitter				
▽ Slider	9.4%	83.9 [97]	-4.7 [99]	-36.1 [91]
◇ Curveball	0.1%	77.8 [98]	-6.8 [96]	-55.5 [83]
✪ Slow Curveball				
✳ Knuckleball				
▼ Screwball				

Daniel Zamora LHP

Born: 04/15/93 Age: 26 Bats: L Throws: L
Height: 6'3" Weight: 195 Origin: Round 40, 2015 Draft (#1207 overall)

YEAR	TEAM	LVL	AGE	W	L	SV	G	GS	IP	H	HR	BB/9	K/9	K	GB%	BABIP
2016	WVA	A	23	3	2	1	21	0	39	32	2	3.5	10.4	45	47%	.294
2017	BRD	A+	24	2	4	9	37	0	53^1	48	2	2.9	10.3	61	57%	.324
2018	BIN	AA	25	1	1	2	40	1	51^2	37	3	2.8	12.0	69	46%	.291
2018	NYN	MLB	25	1	0	0	16	0	9	6	1	3.0	16.0	16	44%	.333
2019	NYN	MLB	26	2	2	0	41	0	43	39	5	4.0	10.0	49	44%	.296

Breakout: 15% Improve: 23% Collapse: 9% Attrition: 21% MLB: 35%
Comparables: Pat Venditte, Tyler Sturdevant, Rob Wooten

There was an upside to the Mets' complete bullpen breakdown in 2018: desperation occasionally breeds opportunity for the unheralded. Few players who played as well as Zamora did at the end of the season were as anonymous heading into the year, but the funky left-hander has forced his way into the Mets' 2019 plans. He's ostensibly a lefty specialist on the strength of his only plus pitch—a frisbee slider that he throws frequently and in all counts. It's possible that a longer look at Zamora might allow opposing hitters to size up his breaker and sit on his below-average fastball, but the Stony Brook product has had statistical success at every level so far. Why should the big leagues be any different?

YEAR	TEAM	LVL	AGE	WHIP	ERA	DRA	WARP	MPH	FB%	WHF	CSP
2016	WVA	A	23	1.21	3.46	2.96	0.8				
2017	BRD	A+	24	1.22	1.86	2.78	1.3				
2018	BIN	AA	25	1.03	3.48	2.52	1.5				
2018	NYN	MLB	25	1.00	3.00	2.26	0.3	90.9	21.5	15.2	51.4
2019	NYN	MLB	26	1.33	3.97	4.36	0.2	90.5	21.9	15.5	52.3

Daniel Zamora, continued

	Pitch Shape vs LHH	Pitch Shape vs RHH
	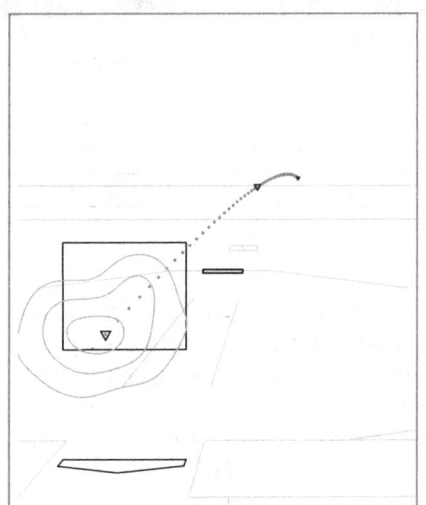	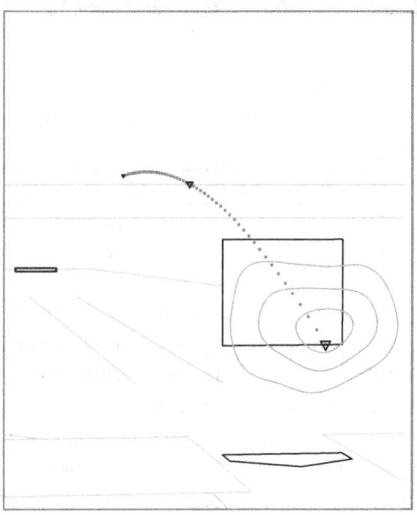

Type	Frequency	Velocity	H Movement	V Movement
● Fastball	21.5%	89.3 [90]	6 [103]	-21.1 [83]
☐ Sinker				
+ Cutter				
▲ Changeup				
✕ Splitter				
▽ Slider	78.5%	78.7 [74]	-15.8 [147]	-41.2 [76]
◇ Curveball				
⊕ Slow Curveball				
✱ Knuckleball				
▼ Screwball				

Pete Alonso 1B

Born: 12/07/94 Age: 24 Bats: R Throws: R
Height: 6'3" Weight: 245 Origin: Round 2, 2016 Draft (#64 overall)

YEAR	TEAM	LVL	AGE	PA	R	2B	3B	HR	RBI	BB	K	SB	CS	AVG/OBP/SLG
2016	BRO	A-	21	123	20	12	1	5	21	11	22	0	1	.321/.382/.587
2017	SLU	A+	22	346	45	23	0	16	58	25	64	3	4	.286/.361/.516
2017	BIN	AA	22	47	7	4	1	2	5	2	7	0	0	.311/.340/.578
2018	BIN	AA	23	273	42	12	0	15	52	43	50	0	2	.314/.440/.573
2018	LVG	AAA	23	301	50	19	1	21	67	33	78	0	1	.260/.355/.585
2019	NYN	MLB	24	358	46	17	1	18	51	36	99	0	0	.220/.310/.452

Breakout: 25% Improve: 43% Collapse: 9% Attrition: 25% MLB: 69%
Comparables: Rhys Hoskins, Chris Carter, A.J. Reed

When you hit at every level in the minor leagues, at some point you have to look past any flaws and give a man a chance. So nevermind that Alonso is a right-handed first baseman with little defensive value and no flexibility; he led the minor leagues in homers last season after ripping up both the Eastern and Pacific Coast League. By mid-season, it became fairly well-established that the former Gator was the best first baseman in the system, and that didn't just include rival prospect Dom Smith. The lack of a September call-up audibly frustrated Alonso, who took out his aggression on a few pitchers in the Arizona Fall League where he hit another half-dozen dingers. While there are precious few right-right first basemen worthy of everyday playing time at the game's highest level, Alonso has made it clear that he deserves his shot as a starter in 2019.

YEAR	TEAM	LVL	AGE	PA	DRC+	VORP	BABIP	BRR	FRAA	WARP
2016	BRO	A-	21	123	179	14.1	.357	-0.5	1B(27): 2.3	0.9
2017	SLU	A+	22	346	158	11.8	.314	-5.8	1B(78): 3.2	1.4
2017	BIN	AA	22	47	104	3.3	.333	-0.1	1B(5): 0.1	0.0
2018	BIN	AA	23	273	177	30.5	.344	-1.6	1B(51): 1.8	2.2
2018	LVG	AAA	23	301	122	14.6	.284	1.2	1B(59): 5.0	1.4
2019	NYN	MLB	24	358	108	10.2	.253	-0.8	1B 2	1.2

Travis d'Arnaud C

Born: 02/10/89 Age: 30 Bats: R Throws: R
Height: 6'2" Weight: 210 Origin: Round 1, 2007 Draft (#37 overall)

YEAR	TEAM	LVL	AGE	PA	R	2B	3B	HR	RBI	BB	K	SB	CS	AVG/OBP/SLG
2016	NYN	MLB	27	276	27	7	0	4	15	19	50	0	0	.247/.307/.323
2017	NYN	MLB	28	376	39	19	1	16	57	23	59	0	0	.244/.293/.443
2018	NYN	MLB	29	16	1	0	0	1	3	1	5	0	0	.200/.250/.400
2019	NYN	MLB	30	234	25	10	1	6	25	17	41	0	0	.249/.309/.390

Breakout: 1% Improve: 41% Collapse: 18% Attrition: 10% MLB: 94%
Comparables: Ramon Hernandez, Josh Bard, Michael Barrett

d'Arnaud's career has been one of qualified compliments—he's a good hitter *for a catcher*, or he's a potential All-Star *if he can stay healthy*—but now he'll likely never qualify for a big-league batting title. This go-round, it took just four games before he tore his UCL and knocked himself out for the season, out of the Mets' future plans and potentially out of a career behind the dish. Now what? His steady job is gone. His 20s are toast. And the position that granted him so much value is at risk, if not missing in action. If his patience and power haven't faded, then some squad will give him another chance once he hits free agency after the 2019 season. If he can resume a role as a backstop, his framing skills will make him valuable when he plays. But, for now, d'Arnaud will attempt to stay healthy in a supporting role and just doing that would qualify as a success at this point.

YEAR	TEAM	P. COUNT	FRM RUNS	BLK RUNS	THRW RUNS	TOT RUNS
2016	NYN	10281	8.1	1.0	-2.5	6.2
2017	NYN	13404	11.2	0.9	-3.1	9.0
2018	NYN	689	1.0	0.1	0.0	1.0
2019	NYN	7225	5.4	0.5	-1.2	4.9

YEAR	TEAM	LVL	AGE	PA	DRC+	VORP	BABIP	BRR	FRAA	WARP
2016	NYN	MLB	27	276	80	6.2	.293	-0.3	C(73): 8.2	1.5
2017	NYN	MLB	28	376	99	15.8	.250	-2.2	C(93): 11.5, 2B(1): 0.0	2.7
2018	NYN	MLB	29	16	80	0.6	.222	-0.1	C(4): 1.0	0.1
2019	NYN	MLB	30	234	89	6.9	.280	-0.4	C 5	1.1

Andres Gimenez SS

Born: 09/04/98 Age: 20 Bats: L Throws: R
Height: 5'11" Weight: 161 Origin: International Free Agent, 2015

YEAR	TEAM	LVL	AGE	PA	R	2B	3B	HR	RBI	BB	K	SB	CS	AVG/OBP/SLG
2016	MET	RK	17	141	24	10	4	1	17	21	13	7	1	.360/.461/.544
2016	DME	RK	17	134	28	10	0	2	21	25	9	6	7	.340/.478/.500
2017	COL	A	18	399	50	9	4	4	31	28	61	14	8	.265/.346/.349
2018	SLU	A+	19	351	43	20	4	6	30	22	70	28	11	.282/.348/.432
2018	BIN	AA	19	153	19	9	1	0	16	9	22	10	3	.277/.344/.358
2019	NYN	MLB	20	251	29	7	1	5	19	11	56	9	3	.189/.245/.293

Breakout: 18% Improve: 19% Collapse: 0% Attrition: 4% MLB: 19%
Comparables: J.P. Crawford, Francisco Lindor, Elvis Andrus

Arguably the best prospect in the Mets' system, Gimenez isn't so much a star as he is a constellation; the whole surpasses the sum of the parts. He's possessed of many tiny points of light: the brightest might be the beginnings of a plus hit tool and better-than-average speed. Every piece of the picture matters. There's average leather at shortstop that could play up if he moves to second base, a hint at double-digit home-run power and a decidedly advanced approach for a guy who spent all of 2018 playing in both High-A and Double-A at 19 years old. If one light goes out, he could just be a utility player; if two dim, then he may not make it out of the minors. But if he continues on this path, the sky's the limit.

YEAR	TEAM	LVL	AGE	PA	DRC+	VORP	BABIP	BRR	FRAA	WARP
2016	MET	RK	17	141	192	28.1	.388	2.1	SS(29): 7.1	2.4
2016	DME	RK	17	134	191	20.0	.344	-0.9	SS(19): -2.9, 2B(12): -1.1	1.0
2017	COL	A	18	399	110	22.5	.310	0.7	SS(89): 6.6	2.2
2018	SLU	A+	19	351	112	24.9	.343	3.4	SS(83): 14.2, 2B(2): -0.1	3.1
2018	BIN	AA	19	153	101	8.4	.330	1.2	SS(36): -1.3, 2B(1): 0.2	0.4
2019	NYN	MLB	20	251	44	-6.7	.225	0.6	SS 3, 2B 0	-0.4

Ronny Mauricio SS

Born: 04/04/01   Age: 18   Bats: B   Throws: R
Height: 6'3"   Weight: 166   Origin: International Free Agent, 2017

YEAR	TEAM	LVL	AGE	PA	R	2B	3B	HR	RBI	BB	K	SB	CS	AVG/OBP/SLG
2018	MTS	RK	17	212	26	13	3	3	31	10	31	1	6	.279/.307/.421
2018	KNG	RK	17	35	6	3	0	0	4	3	9	1	0	.233/.286/.333
2019	*NYN*	*MLB*	*18*	*251*	*13*	*9*	*0*	*4*	*20*	*7*	*88*	*0*	*0*	*.121/.144/.211*

Comparables: Adalberto Mondesi, Wilmer Flores, Tommy Brown

1. Mauricio has so much raw talent—he's a switch-hitting middle infielder that flashes power—that Lin-Manuel Miranda probably looks to *him* for inspiration.

2. Mauricio is just as likely to stick at shortstop—he's already 6'3"-6'4" and growing—as he is to get struck by lightning while getting eaten by a shark. *(Note that since he plays for the Mets, this is a legitimate, if unlikely, injury possibility.)*

3. Mauricio is so young—he played most of 2018 in the Gulf Coast League as a 17-year-old—that he's been around for less time than Outkast's *Stankonia*.

4. Mauricio is so far away from the majors that NASA just underwent a mission to land an unmanned probe on him.

YEAR	TEAM	LVL	AGE	PA	DRC+	VORP	BABIP	BRR	FRAA	WARP
2018	MTS	RK	17	212	124	10.1	.310	-0.3	SS(45): 0.3	0.7
2018	KNG	RK	17	35	74	1.9	.304	0.5	SS(8): -0.1	0.0
2019	*NYN*	*MLB*	*18*	*251*	*-14*	*-25.4*	*.162*	*-0.6*	*SS 1*	*-2.7*

Shervyen Newton SS
Born: 04/24/99 Age: 20 Bats: B Throws: R
Height: 6'4" Weight: 180 Origin: International Free Agent, 2015

YEAR	TEAM	LVL	AGE	PA	R	2B	3B	HR	RBI	BB	K	SB	CS	AVG/OBP/SLG
2016	MET	RK	17	150	18	5	1	0	5	22	32	0	5	.169/.347/.229
2017	MET	RK	18	303	51	11	9	1	31	50	57	10	4	.311/.433/.444
2018	KNG	RK	19	266	50	16	2	5	41	46	84	4	0	.280/.408/.449
2019	NYN	MLB	20	251	21	5	1	5	17	22	91	0	0	.120/.198/.214

Breakout: 3% Improve: 3% Collapse: 0% Attrition: 1% MLB: 3%
Comparables: Tyler Wade, Tim Beckham, Amed Rosario

After a couple of years getting his bearings in the Dominican Summer League, Newton came stateside in 2018 and impressed during his first taste of American pro ball. The numbers in Kingsport were fine, but the tools stand out; along with a tall, lean frame, the big infielder has lightning-quick bat speed fueling his legit raw power, and he can take a hack from both sides of the plate. In part because he shared a diamond with fellow high-test prospects Ronny Mauricio and Mark Vientos, Newton spent a fair amount of time at second base, despite currently fitting in as a shortstop and perhaps lining up at the hot corner sometime in the future. He'll have every opportunity to figure out off-speed pitches—the kryptonite of so many young hitters—given the abundance of tools in his profile.

YEAR	TEAM	LVL	AGE	PA	DRC+	VORP	BABIP	BRR	FRAA	WARP
2016	MET	RK	17	150	97	3.6	.233	-1.2	SS(18): -0.5, 3B(11): -0.4	0.1
2017	MET	RK	18	303	163	33.9	.398	-2.0	SS(60): 7.7, 3B(5): 0.8	3.3
2018	KNG	RK	19	266	130	24.4	.421	2.2	SS(49): 10.8, 2B(3): 0.3	2.3
2019	NYN	MLB	20	251	16	-16.3	.166	-0.3	SS 3, 2B 0	-1.4

Mark Vientos 3B
Born: 12/11/99   Age: 19   Bats: R   Throws: R
Height: 6'4"   Weight: 185   Origin: Round 2, 2017 Draft (#59 overall)

YEAR	TEAM	LVL	AGE	PA	R	2B	3B	HR	RBI	BB	K	SB	CS	AVG/OBP/SLG
2017	MTS	RK	17	193	22	12	0	4	24	14	42	0	2	.259/.316/.397
2018	KNG	RK	18	262	32	12	0	11	52	37	43	1	0	.287/.389/.489
2019	NYN	MLB	19	251	21	6	0	9	28	18	73	0	0	.148/.208/.295

Breakout: 5%   Improve: 7%   Collapse: 0%   Attrition: 3%   MLB: 10%
Comparables: Rafael Devers, Gleyber Torres, Nomar Mazara

The Mets have a predilection for moving their position player prospects slowly through the ranks, so it wasn't exactly a surprise that Vientos spent the entire year at Kingsport despite proving he was more than capable against the throwers at the level. It also wasn't a surprise that the young Floridian hit for power, displayed a mature approach at the plate, and acquitted himself well in his first full season at third base; the former second-round draft pick had first-round talent from the jump. The shocks may come more as he progresses through full-season ball, as he'll need to catch up to premium velocity better, but he could force the Mets into promoting him more aggressively if the offensive barrage continues.

YEAR	TEAM	LVL	AGE	PA	DRC+	VORP	BABIP	BRR	FRAA	WARP
2017	MTS	RK	17	193	108	8.2	.313	0.8	SS(19): -1.6, 3B(14): 0.1	0.0
2018	KNG	RK	18	262	149	17.4	.312	-3.0	3B(54): -1.7	0.7
2019	NYN	MLB	19	251	31	-15.6	.165	-0.6	3B -1	-1.8

New York Mets 2019

Eric Hanhold   RHP

Born: 11/01/93   Age: 25   Bats: R   Throws: R
Height: 6'5"   Weight: 220   Origin: Round 6, 2015 Draft (#181 overall)

YEAR	TEAM	LVL	AGE	W	L	SV	G	GS	IP	H	HR	BB/9	K/9	K	GB%	BABIP
2016	BRV	A+	22	2	12	0	19	19	101	120	12	2.9	5.7	64	54%	.327
2017	CAR	A+	23	8	3	2	30	3	64	71	3	3.0	8.4	60	60%	.364
2018	BIN	AA	24	3	1	8	17	0	25.1	21	1	3.2	11.4	32	60%	.323
2018	LVG	AAA	24	2	2	0	14	0	19	25	1	3.3	9.5	20	49%	.429
2018	NYN	MLB	24	0	0	0	3	0	2.1	4	0	3.9	7.7	2	33%	.444
2019	NYN	MLB	25	1	1	0	15	0	16.1	15	2	4.0	9.2	17	50%	.299

Breakout: 5%   Improve: 8%   Collapse: 6%   Attrition: 12%   MLB: 16%
Comparables: Jeremy Horst, Ryan O'Rourke, Dan Meyer

You might wonder why a guy with a 7.11 ERA over just 19 innings in Triple-A might be called up to a major-league bullpen role, but this is the Mets we're talking about. Not only was the team in desperate need of middle relief efficacy, but Hanhold's numbers distract from some solid underlying sparkles. His fastball comes in hard and has good movement, and at its best it can get both grounders and whiffs; much of his difficulty in Vegas seemed to spawn from a ridiculous BABIP over a short stretch. Though an early-season oblique injury slowed him down and a late-season recurrence prevented him from logging more innings with the big club in September, he's likely to pop back up with the Mets as they revamp their 'pen for 2019.

YEAR	TEAM	LVL	AGE	WHIP	ERA	DRA	WARP	MPH	FB%	WHF	CSP
2016	BRV	A+	22	1.51	4.81	5.55	-0.1				
2017	CAR	A+	23	1.44	3.94	4.03	0.7				
2018	BIN	AA	24	1.18	2.84	2.89	0.6				
2018	LVG	AAA	24	1.68	7.11	3.24	0.4				
2018	NYN	MLB	24	2.14	7.71	8.70	-0.1	96.7	71.2	6.8	46.1
2019	NYN	MLB	25	1.39	4.10	4.47	0.1	96.4	72.9	6.9	47.2

Franklyn Kilome   RHP

Born: 06/25/95   Age: 24   Bats: R   Throws: R
Height: 6'6"   Weight: 175   Origin: International Free Agent, 2013

YEAR	TEAM	LVL	AGE	W	L	SV	G	GS	IP	H	HR	BB/9	K/9	K	GB%	BABIP
2016	LWD	A	21	5	8	0	23	23	114^2	113	6	3.9	10.2	130	49%	.346
2017	CLR	A+	22	6	4	0	19	19	97^1	96	5	3.4	7.7	83	48%	.325
2017	REA	AA	22	1	3	0	5	5	29^2	25	2	4.6	6.1	20	43%	.267
2018	REA	AA	23	4	6	0	19	19	102	96	7	4.5	7.3	83	46%	.305
2018	BIN	AA	23	0	3	0	7	7	38	31	3	2.4	9.9	42	41%	.289
2019	NYN	MLB	24	7	8	0	22	22	115^1	107	15	4.2	8.8	112	42%	.305

Breakout: 4%   Improve: 5%   Collapse: 6%   Attrition: 12%   MLB: 17%
Comparables: Scott Barlow, Caleb Smith, James Houser

Since 2017, the Mets' stock-in-trade has been dealing big-league parts for middling relief arms in the hopes of stabilizing a shaky bullpen (not working!) and saving cash (working!) When the Mets pried Kilome loose from the Phillies in exchange for Asdrubal Cabrera last year, the fanbase seemed to breathe a sigh of relief. *Finally.* After all, Kilome was a top-100 prospect and a pitcher with legitimate middle-of-the-rotation upside. Sure, he's aging out of prospectdom and he'd worn out his welcome in a stacked Philadelphia farm system, but he has plus velocity on his fastball and a solid second offering in his curve. The stats haven't quite matched the projection as of yet, but there's real hope that Kilome could emerge as a legitimate starter in 2019. Or rather, there was that hope. During the World Series, the Mets announced that Kilome has become a true Met: he'll have Tommy John surgery and miss the 2019 season.

YEAR	TEAM	LVL	AGE	WHIP	ERA	DRA	WARP	MPH	FB%	WHF	CSP
2016	LWD	A	21	1.42	3.85	3.14	2.6				
2017	CLR	A+	22	1.37	2.59	4.55	0.8				
2017	REA	AA	22	1.35	3.64	4.00	0.4				
2018	REA	AA	23	1.44	4.24	4.65	0.8				
2018	BIN	AA	23	1.08	4.03	4.50	0.4				
2019	NYN	MLB	24	1.40	4.57	5.28	0.0				

David Peterson LHP

Born: 09/03/95 Age: 23 Bats: L Throws: L
Height: 6'6" Weight: 240 Origin: Round 1, 2017 Draft (#20 overall)

YEAR	TEAM	LVL	AGE	W	L	SV	G	GS	IP	H	HR	BB/9	K/9	K	GB%	BABIP
2018	COL	A	22	1	4	0	9	9	59^1	46	1	1.7	8.6	57	68%	.283
2018	SLU	A+	22	6	6	0	13	13	68^2	74	1	2.5	7.6	58	64%	.335
2019	NYN	MLB	23	6	6	0	17	17	91^1	86	10	3.2	8.0	82	52%	.304

Breakout: 7%   Improve: 18%   Collapse: 12%   Attrition: 20%   MLB: 36%
Comparables: Sal Romano, Brian Flynn, Fernando Romero

As a college left-handed pitcher who was drafted in the first round, there's no reason Peterson shouldn't be chewing up hitters in the low minors as he barrels toward his true test in the upper echelons of minor league baseball. Instead, the Mets have moved methodically with him, starting his 2018 in Columbia before finally moving him to a more appropriate level at St. Lucie. While the tall lefty managed to maintain his incredible ground-ball rate at the more advanced level, he didn't put up the strikeout numbers one would hope for from a top-tier pitching prospect. You can chalk that up to his mediocre fastball, or maybe even his slow burn through the minors, but there's still a fair chance Peterson could become a reliable mid-rotation lefty or a LOOGY before it's all said and done.

YEAR	TEAM	LVL	AGE	WHIP	ERA	DRA	WARP	MPH	FB%	WHF	CSP
2018	COL	A	22	0.96	1.82	3.50	1.2				
2018	SLU	A+	22	1.35	4.33	3.99	1.1				
2019	NYN	MLB	23	1.30	4.08	4.70	0.6				

LINEOUTS

Hitters

HITTER	POS	TEAM	LVL	AGE	PA	R	2B	3B	HR	RBI	BB	K	SB	CS	AVG/OBP/SLG	DRC+	WARP
Gregor Blanco	CF	SAC	AAA	34	194	20	7	2	4	13	23	40	2	1	.247/.337/.382	98	-0.9
	CF	SFN	MLB	34	203	19	7	3	2	12	12	58	6	2	.217/.262/.317	60	-0.7
Keon Broxton	CF	CSP	AAA	28	334	47	16	2	10	37	30	119	27	4	.254/.323/.421	82	0.6
	CF	MIL	MLB	28	89	15	2	2	4	11	11	28	5	1	.179/.281/.410	77	0.5
Gavin Cecchini	2B	LVG	AAA	24	119	14	11	1	2	9	7	15	1	1	.294/.342/.468	99	0.0
Carlos Cortes	2B	BRO	A-	21	202	26	5	2	4	24	17	34	1	0	.264/.338/.382	141	0.6
Braxton Lee	CF	MIA	MLB	24	18	0	0	0	0	2	1	8	0	0	.176/.222/.176	58	-0.1
	CF	JUP	A+	24	29	6	0	0	0	3	3	3	0	1	.292/.393/.292	116	-0.2
	CF	JAX	AA	24	127	16	6	0	1	7	16	19	3	1	.218/.315/.300	101	0.5
	CF	NWO	AAA	24	201	24	6	2	0	9	19	37	4	6	.235/.307/.291	61	-0.8
Desmond Lindsay	OF	SLU	A+	21	335	27	11	5	3	30	37	89	7	7	.218/.310/.320	86	0.4
Ali Sanchez	C	COL	A	21	205	26	11	1	4	22	10	23	1	1	.259/.293/.389	119	1.0
	C	SLU	A+	21	142	11	9	0	2	16	5	15	1	1	.274/.296/.385	98	0.1
Tim Tebow	LF	BIN	AA	30	298	32	14	1	6	36	22	103	1	0	.273/.336/.399	101	-0.8

Just 16 years old, **Francisco Alvarez** is already 5'11", 220 pounds, and a multi-millionaire. After receiving the largest bonus in Mets international signing history, this young Venezuelan "catcher" will have a decade to learn how to improve his receiving game and tap into his substantial raw power. ⚾ A minor-league free agent find before 2012, **Gregor Blanco** saved a perfect game, caught the final out of a no-hitter and contributed to two World Series championships. If this is the end, he's enjoyed a dream career for a fourth outfielder, and a bright future in coaching awaits him. ⚾ **Keon Broxton**'s incredible week between late June and early July should be entered as a candidate for the Ultimate Replacement Player (URP) leaderboard. Broxton demonstrated phenomenal game-saving defense while adding a few extra base hits for good measure. ⚾ Is it fair to say that his early-season foot injury derailed **Gavin Cecchini**'s forward progress, or was that already a lost cause despite solid numbers in his most recent Vegas go-round? Either way, he doesn't look like much of a major leaguer either at the dish or in the field. ⚾ Recent third-round pick **Carlos Cortes** is both positionally dexterous and bilaterally ambidextrous: he throws left-handed when playing the infield and right-handed when playing the outfield. He packs some power in his diminutive frame, but he'll need a lot of polish before cracking a major-league roster. ⚾ **Braxton Lee** has received a decent amount of hype at various points along the way, but the Marlins declined to protect him from the *minor-league* phase of the Rule 5 draft. The Mets snatched him up, but that just means he'll be playing for a new Triple-A team in 2019. ⚾ Toolsy center fielder **Desmond Lindsay** is a lot like that film project that you saw on Kickstarter that looks amazing but you know will never hit its funding goal. ⓧ The *T.J.* in **T.J. Rivera** doesn't stand for "Tommy John," but it might as well. The eponymous surgery cost him the entire 2018 season, during which he saw Jeff McNeil basically doppelgang his 2017 breakout and push him down the org's depth chart. ⓧ Catching prospect **Ali Sanchez** tried out the Florida State League and the Arizona Fall League in 2018, but didn't impress much in either showing. He's got the glove for his position, but his bat is purely holographic. ⓧ Everything about the **Tim Tebow** Experience is vaguely surreal: he's a college football analyst who suits up for a team called the Rumble Ponies, draws large crowds of fans and admirers and hits just well enough to be a league-average hitter in the Eastern League.

Pitchers

PITCHER	TEAM	LVL	AGE	W	L	SV	G	GS	IP	H	HR	BB/9	K/9	K	GB%	WHIP	ERA	DRA	WARP
P.J. Conlon	NYN	MLB	24	0	0	0	3	2	7^2	15	2	2.3	5.9	5	29%	2.22	8.22	7.88	-0.2
	LVG	AAA	24	4	9	0	23	21	114	147	20	3.1	6.5	82	36%	1.63	6.55	5.40	0.2
Chris Flexen	NYN	MLB	23	0	2	0	4	1	6^1	14	2	8.5	4.3	3	40%	3.16	12.79	7.44	-0.2
	LVG	AAA	23	6	7	0	18	17	92	109	11	3.0	7.6	78	43%	1.52	4.40	5.11	0.4
Anthony Kay	COL	A	23	4	4	0	13	13	69^1	73	6	2.9	10.1	78	45%	1.37	4.54	4.00	1.0
	SLU	A+	23	3	7	0	10	10	53^1	51	1	4.6	7.6	45	41%	1.46	3.88	4.21	0.7
Walker Lockett	SDN	MLB	24	0	3	0	4	3	15	22	4	6.0	7.2	12	56%	2.13	9.60	6.05	-0.1
	ELP	AAA	24	5	9	0	23	23	133^1	145	17	2.2	8.0	118	48%	1.34	4.72	4.18	2.1
Timothy Peterson	LVG	AAA	27	0	1	8	32	0	38^2	29	4	2.3	12.8	55	38%	1.01	3.49	3.11	0.9
	NYN	MLB	27	2	2	0	22	0	27^2	29	8	1.6	8.1	25	34%	1.23	6.18	5.51	-0.2
Jacob Rhame	LVG	AAA	25	1	2	11	25	0	32^1	22	4	2.2	11.4	41	32%	0.93	3.06	3.42	0.6
	NYN	MLB	25	1	2	1	30	0	32^1	38	8	2.2	7.8	28	30%	1.42	5.85	4.84	0.0
Ryder Ryan	SLU	A+	23	1	0	2	16	0	20^1	14	0	2.2	10.2	23	47%	0.93	1.77	2.66	0.5
	BIN	AA	23	3	3	3	26	0	32^2	27	5	2.8	9.9	36	38%	1.13	4.13	2.85	0.8
Drew Smith	LVG	AAA	24	5	1	2	23	1	32^2	26	3	3.3	8.3	30	46%	1.16	2.76	7.42	-0.8
	NYN	MLB	24	1	1	0	27	0	28	34	2	1.9	5.8	18	39%	1.43	3.54	5.07	0.0
Stephen Villines	COL	A	22	2	4	6	24	0	33^1	33	2	1.4	14.6	54	46%	1.14	4.86	2.88	0.8
	SLU	A+	22	2	0	4	16	0	22	7	0	2.5	10.2	25	44%	0.59	0.41	2.99	0.5
	BIN	AA	22	1	0	0	7	0	11^1	6	1	1.6	13.5	17	39%	0.71	3.18	3.65	0.2
Simeon Woods-Richardson	MTS	Rk	17	1	0	1	5	2	11^1	9	0	3.2	11.9	15	50%	1.15	0.00	3.39	0.3
	KNG	Rk	17	0	0	0	2	2	6	6	1	0.0	16.5	11	38%	1.00	4.50	3.92	0.1

Belfast-born **P.J. Conlon** came up with the woeful Mets, but was spirited away to the contending Dodgers on a waiver claim for four glorious days before being re-acquired by the Amazins. Perhaps the "luck of the Irish" only applies to leprechauns, and not LOOGYs. ⓧ It was hard to imagine that **Chris Flexen** could follow up an abysmal showing as the Mets' emergency starter in 2017 with an even worse 2018. Unfortunately, we don't need to imagine it—the homer-prone starter was throttled in a brief major-league cameo and looks to be stuck in the minors. ⓧ Signed as potential rotation depth, **A.J. Griffin** gave up 16 runs in three innings at Triple-A and the Mets released him before April had ended. The California native likely ends his pro career not with a whimper, but rather several resounding bangs. ⓧ **Chris Hatcher** gave up a three-run walk-off dinger to Taylor Ward in the A's last regular-season game of 2018. It can't get *worse*, so why not keep pitching? ⓧ Right-handed out machine **Jordan Humphreys** was having a nice low-minors breakout in 2017 before UCL surgery derailed his 2018 season. If his plus command comes back in 2019, he could quickly rise up both pref lists and minor league levels to catch up with his contemporaries. ⓧ Left-hander **Anthony Kay** made his pro debut in 2018, and put up solid numbers in a season split between Columbus and St. Lucie. Despite a solid changeup, he probably doesn't project as more than a back-of-the-rotation arm. ⓧ **Walker Lockett**'s stuff and command are both at a point where if the other was slightly better, he could be a viable back-end starter. As they're each a little short, he's probably an up-and-down guy. ⓧ Things went great for **Timothy Peterson**—whose eighth season in the Mets' organization was his first in which he cracked the majors—up until the calendar turned to July. From that point on, the command-and-control righty reliever gave up dinger after dinger and pitched his way back into a Triple-A role. ⓧ Somehow young fireballer **Jacob Rhame** spent exactly 32.1 innings thriving as closer for the Las Vegas 51s and exactly 32 1/3 innings getting shelled under better pitching conditions in Flushing. Perhaps it had something to do with the fact that he had *10* different stints with the big-league team; he went up and down so fast and frequently you'd think he was a Duncan Imperial. ⓧ Like almost every other relief prospect, **Ryder Ryan** has a mid-90s fastball and a potential plus slider. Maybe he'll be able to give his future bullpen-mate Edwin Diaz some advice about how to deal with the expectations that come with being the centerpiece of a Jay Bruce trade. ⓧ Good surface-level numbers and the ability to limit walks made **Drew Smith** an integral part of the Mets' late-season bullpen. The bad news? Smith hasn't shown enough underlying stuff to make him an integral part of a *good* team's bullpen. ⓧ When we last saw **Thomas Szapucki**, he was mowing down low-minors hitters with three interesting pitches and serious heat coming off the left side. Of course, that was right after a shoulder injury and right before Tommy John surgery, so 2019 will be a watershed year for his top-prospect status. ⓧ Over the past two years, former Jayhawk **Stephen Villines** has pitched 94 innings of pro ball, and in that time struck out 137 and walked just 14. Don't be shocked if he brings his low arm slot, pinpoint control and American Legion velocity to Queens as a situational reliever very soon. ⓧ If **Simeon Woods-Richardson** was a filet, you'd send him back; he's that raw. Fortunately he's not a steak, he's a high-potential right-handed pitcher with a four-pitch arsenal, solid velocity and a nice start to his pro career. No one's sending him back.

Mets Prospects

The State of the System:
What if I told you there was an entire prospect list made out of our low minors sleepers superlative?

The Top Ten:

1 Andres Gimenez SS OFP: 60 Likely: 55
ETA: September 2019 or earlier
Born: 09/04/98   Age: 20   Bats: L   Throws: R   Height: 5'11"   Weight: 161
Origin: International Free Agent, 2015

The Report: Gimenez showed up this spring in better shape, shed some baby fat, and added athleticism to his polished up-the-middle profile. The 19-year-old hit at both High-A and Double-A, and his plus hit tool projection backs up the statline. Gimenez has exceptional bat control, his path keeps the lumber in the zone a long time, and he can adjust in-swing to offspeed. He very well could have seasons where he hits .300. The power at present plays mostly gap-to-gap. The raw is 40 at present, potentially average at physical maturity if he adds good weight to his frame. He has high-end 6 speed and is a smart, aggressive baserunner who could be good for 30 steals a season.

The plus speed plays in the field as well, giving Gimenez above-average range that plays up further due to a good first step. While we previously had concerns about him sticking at the 6, his defense has improved and he checks every box for a potential plus shortstop—good instincts, hands, and actions; smooth around the bag; plus throwing arm. The lack of power projection and his occasional over aggression against offspeed limits the ceiling a bit, but he's as good a bet as any prospect in baseball to have an eight-year major league career of some variety.

The Risks: Low. While the profile lacks superstar upside at present, Gimenez inherits the "safe middle infield prospect" mantle from predecessors Willy Adames and Ozzie Albies. He doesn't have the power upside they've shown, but he's a plus athlete with a good hit tool. If you want to bet on a "high-floor" profile at the 6, that's the one.

Bret Sayre's Fantasy Take: In some ways, this is a test to see if we've learned anything from the army of smaller, hit-tool-first prospects who have reached higher upsides than we would have ever comfortably projected. Gimenez has everything you want, except for the power, but if he can grow into even 15-homer pop, we're looking at someone who could approximate Jean Segura's fantasy value and maintain top-10 shortstop status even if he never really competes with the Lindors or Machados of the world.

2. Pete Alonso 1B

OFP: 60   Likely: 55   ETA: July 2018
Born: 12/07/94   Age: 24   Bats: R   Throws: R   Height: 6'3"   Weight: 245
Origin: Round 2, 2016 Draft (#64 overall)

The Report: Listen, we hate this profile as a rule. This is a R/R college first baseman who is a cover model for the BIG BOY SZN catalog and he doesn't play great or even particularly good defense. You will go absolutely broke betting on players of this type to make it. But some do, and we think Pete Alonso is going to be one of the exceptions.

We said last year that 2018 would be a big year for Alonso. He killed Double-A for the first half of the season, did the same in Triple-A from mid-July on after a slow first month, and impressed in the Arizona Fall League. We said he projected for plus game power with a chance for more. Thirty-six homers in the high-minors later, the chance got there, and he now projects for 80 game power. We said Dom Smith might establish himself in the majors first and cloud up Alonso's profile and, well, pretty much the exact opposite of that happened. He's got power, he's got patience, he's got bat speed, he can turn on velocity, he's got better feel for contact than you usually see in these types of players.

It's not all roses, obviously; he'd be ahead of Gimenez if it was. Outside of the Vladitos of the world, you don't know when a guy is going to be able to hit major league sliders until you know, and we don't know yet. The Mets left him in the minors all year, whether because of service time or 40-man considerations or a veteran fetish, robbing us of the chance to know. He's still, generously, a work-in-progress with the glove at first base, although he ranges and throws well enough. We believe that he's "playable bad" there instead of "needs to be traded to the American League," but there are scouts who project the latter.

The Risks: Low-to-medium, depending on how you look at it. There's low risk in the tools, he's about as fully-formed as a prospect can be, in part because he shouldn't be prospect-eligible. There's still substantial risk in the profile until we see how good he is at getting on base against MLB pitching. There isn't a ton separating Rhys Hoskins and C.J. Cron in profile or skills, but that slight gap is the difference between a star and a waiver claim. Mets fans might also cringe at the exit velocity hype after The Eric Campbell Experience.

Bret Sayre's Fantasy Take: Frankly, I'm shocked Brendan let me write this. It's not that my favorite player growing up was Howard Johnson, or that I can still remember exactly where I was when Todd Pratt hit the walkoff homer that sent the Mets to the NLCS in 1999 (the percussion building of the old Sam Ash in midtown Manhattan.) It's that I've been subscribing to BIG BOY SZN for over a decade now. I own a Dan Vogelbach Cubs shirsey unironically. This profile weakens me, and although guidance counselors and career advisors alike will tell you to identify your weaknesses so that you can overcome them, that implies you want to overcome them. So yes I'm on board with Alonso as a top-10 dynasty prospect, and yes I'm on board with Alonso as a 40-homer bat, and yes I'm on board with Alonso being a top-200 pick in redraft formats this season. The average isn't going to be special, but he could run it up to .280, which could leave him with an OBP approaching .400.

3. Ronny Mauricio SS OFP: 60 Likely: 50
ETA: 2022 if things go pretty well.
Born: 04/04/01 Age: 18 Bats: B Throws: R Height: 6'3" Weight: 166
Origin: International Free Agent, 2017

The Report: Here's an example of both sides of the coin for ranking J2s. Last year, Jeffrey conceded that Mauricio and Adrian Hernandez—two recently-signed, seven-figure Dominican IFAs with great reports—might both be among the ten best prospects in the system, but we lacked enough information to rank them with any precision, or write anything interesting about them. Mauricio then got nothing but buzz in the spring, earned a stateside assignment, reached the Appy League by the end of the season, and is under consideration for the 101. Hernandez was left in the Dominican complex and played okay in the Dominican Summer League. He's still a prospect too, and he could show up on any Mets list between now and 2025 without surprising us, but this is the last time you'll be reading about him on this particular installment.

As the Seattle trade unfolded, there was a lot made of Jarred Kelenic having the highest upside in this system, but for me, Mauricio is a bigger upside play by more than a little—if less likely to hit it. The body is as projectable as they come. There's plus power potential. There's plus hit tool potential as a switch-hitter. He even might stick at shortstop. In two or three years he could absolutely be a bigger, more physical Andres Gimenez, and that's the makings of a tippy-top global guy. We can dream big right now.

Of course, extreme projectability is as much of a curse as it is a compliment, because it implies considerable rawness. These abilities we're gushing about only come across in flashes and bursts right now. Wilmer Flores had this kind of profile once upon a time, very similar actually, and he turned out pretty well, all things considered. Flores still didn't become a full-time regular in his original org, and didn't make it through his arbitration years without being released.

The Risks: He's played eight games in his career outside of a complex. The body can go in a lot of different directions. Projecting hit tools on players like this is more like talking about Delta Airlines than normal baseball prospect delta. There's star potential, Double-A slugger potential, and every potential in between.

New York Mets 2019

Bret Sayre's Fantasy Take: And just like that we've already hit the flier section of this list. I'm probably going to be one of the higher folks on Mauricio this offseason, mostly because the power projection is a lot of fun, but even I can't squint enough to put him in the discussion for the Top 101 at this point. He should be owned in leagues that roster 200 or more prospects, however.

4. Shervyen Newton   IF   OFP: 60   Likely: 45   ETA: 2022
Born: 04/24/99   Age: 20   Bats: B   Throws: R   Height: 6'4"   Weight: 180
Origin: International Free Agent, 2015

The Report: Newton oozes tools and athleticism. He's 6-foot-4 and lean with a high waist. While only an average runner, he eats up ground with long strides and shows a good second gear. There's at least plus raw power at present and he projects for more down the road. He's a better shortstop than you'd think given the frame. Newton's actions are fluid, his arm's plus, and he has great instincts. He is already a captain of the infield as well. He might simply grow off the position, but he'd be a fine third baseman.

Newton is extremely raw at the plate, but there are positive markers for future development with the bat. He shows plus bat speed with loft, and while he can struggle with spin, especially if you back door it for a strike, he's a pesky hitter who stays in against offspeed and will foul stuff off and work deep counts. He does tend to get pull and lift happy which means he will get beat down in the zone, but there's a potential average hit tool in here with plus game power to go with it. That's a borderline star at shortstop. He also might never hit enough to be more than an up-and-down bench piece. It's rookie ball, man.

The Risks: Extreme. Newton led the Appy League in strikeouts. I'm projecting an average hit tool here, but if he doesn't get there, the profile falls apart a bit. Ditto if he grows off of short. There's a few different ways this can go badly, and they all end with him topping out in Double-A.

Bret Sayre's Fantasy Take: You could basically just copy-and-paste Mauricio's comment here, as Newton carries similar upside and risk with the bat. As alluded to above, there's certainly a path to a .250 average and 30-plus homers by the time the next midterms shake out, with the potential for a more notable value in OBP leagues due to his 2.5-true-outcomes approach at this point in his development. Stay tuned, but stay interested, and make sure he's owned if your league rosters 200 prospects.

5. Mark Vientos   3B   OFP: 55   Likely: 45   ETA: 2022
Born: 12/11/99   Age: 19   Bats: R   Throws: R   Height: 6'4"   Weight: 185
Origin: Round 2, 2017 Draft (#59 overall)

The Report: Vientos was in play for the Mets first pick in the 2017 draft, so they were quite pleased when he was still on the board for their second. Still a few days from turning 19 at publication, Vientos has as much upside in his bat as any prospect in this system due to a plus-plus raw power projection. It's a bit of a length and strength approach at the best of times, and he'll add more length with an occasional hitch in his swing path, but this is the kind of thing that can get smoothed out with time—and something the Mets have had particular success with developmentally. At present though there are swing-and-miss issues, especially on the outer half.

The hit tool is more projectable than you'd think. Vientos shows pretty good feel for contact and has an idea at the plate. He shortens up against better velo and doesn't try to lift and pull everything. In the field he's a bit rough at third base, better on the reaction play than the ones where he has time. The arm is above-average but not a cannon, and he may grow off third base and end up in left field or at first. That would put a lot of pressure on the potential 25+ home run power to actualize.

The Risks: High. Short-season hitter with hit tool and positional questions.

Bret Sayre's Fantasy Take: How many of these same comments are we going to suggest copying and pasting? Vientos could be a 30-homer bat down the road, but he's approximately as far away from the majors as Mauricio and Newton. On the other hand, he showed the best approach of the group, which could lead to more success in full-season ball and a quicker path to the majors. If I had to choose one of these three to run with in a dynasty league right now, it'd be Vientos (though it's close).

David Peterson   LHP   OFP: 55   Likely: 45   ETA: 2020
Born: 09/03/95   Age: 23   Bats: L   Throws: L   Height: 6'6"   Weight: 240
Origin: Round 1, 2017 Draft (#20 overall)

The Report: The Mets were conservative with Peterson in 2018 after a pair of minor injuries in spring training. Despite being a polished college lefty, he finished the season in High-A (we'll return to this theme in a bit). Arguably Peterson's stuff should have overpowered A-ball hitters more than it did. His low-90s fastball comes from a tough angle given his height and slingy, low-three-quarters slot. He pairs it with a very advanced, potential plus slider and commands both offerings well.

The changeup is the clear third pitch at present, and he could use a better armside weapon against righties. Peterson is a massive human, and although there are no real red flags in the delivery past a bit of the usual lefty funk, his body might require some monitoring. Double-A will tell us a lot more about the ultimate profile here, but for now he remains on pace to be a middle or back-end starter, although perhaps not as quickly as you'd have thought when he was drafted.

The Risks: Medium. It's probably low, but I'm hesitant to throw that on any pitching prospect who hasn't seen Double-A yet. Without a changeup grade jump he might fit better in the pen due to platoon issues.

Bret Sayre's Fantasy Take: If you looked up the definition of nondescript potential SP5 in a dictionary—first of all, send me a copy of that dictionary—a picture of Peterson would be right there for all to see. Pitchers like Peterson come off the waiver wire for spells of usefulness upwards of 20 times per season in medium-sized mixed leagues, so use that roster spot on a high-risk hitter who could be a 101 candidate at this time next year.

7. Franklyn Kilome RHP
OFP: 55 Likely: 40 ETA: Late 2019
Born: 06/25/95 Age: 24 Bats: R Throws: R Height: 6'6" Weight: 175
Origin: International Free Agent, 2013

The Report: It gets harder to handwave Kilome's consistency issues now that he's in the upper minors, but on balance his 2018 regular season was at worst a net neutral for his profile. You know the story by now. An easy mid-90s fastball with life up in the zone and heavy down in it. It will flash gloveside cut as well. But sometimes it will just be 90-92, overthrown gloveside for a batter. Sometimes it will be more 92-95 for a start. His curve is a hammer, flashing plus-plus in the low-80s. Kilome sells it like a fastball until it's too late for the batter to do anything other than look foolish.

The search for a third pitch rolls on. The Phillies attempted to teach him a slider for a while, and it still hasn't really taken. It bleeds into the curve too much, just a slurvier version of his 11-6 wipeout downer. Occasionally you'll see one around 85 that is sharp in on lefties, which is a useful different look. A changeup shows itself… occasionally. Kilome has done a better job keeping his mechanics on line since the trade, but there are still a lot of moving parts in both his upper and lower halves, and they can get out of sync, limiting the command projection here to average at best. Then there is the matter of his postseason Tommy John Surgery that will cost him all of 2019. At this point, Kilome might be best served with a move to the pen in 2020.

The Risks: High. This was 6/5 and borderline Top 101 before the UCL tear because we really like the profile, but that was with heavy reliever risk baked in, which is only going up. He will be 25 shortly after he starts throwing meaningful pro innings again, and again, he was riskier than you'd like before he went under the knife.

Bret Sayre's Fantasy Take: I've been along for the ride the last three years, but surgery and a likely reliever future is enough to get me off the bandwagon. Even if the stuff returns, his realistic ceiling at this point is a really good setup option in front of newly-acquired closer Edwin Diaz.

8. Thomas Szapucki LHP
OFP: 55 Likely: 40 ETA: 2020-2021
Born: 06/12/96 Age: 23 Bats: R Throws: L Height: 6'2" Weight: 181
Origin: Round 5, 2015 Draft (#149 overall)

The Report: I really considered recycling last year's report here in full. After Tommy John surgery in summer 2017, Szapucki spent the entire 2018 season rehabbing in the complex.

When healthy, Szapucki has shown a lively fastball in the mid-90s, touching higher, and a big, already-plus hook. He's also flashed a useful change. That's a big, big stuff profile for a lefty. The command profile and repeatability are good for his level of rawness, but he looked pretty raw when he last pitched. Things like fielding, holding runners, and throwing to bases were all issues, and his delivery is unorthodox; this is, conveniently, the type of stuff you can work on while rehabbing. So is changeup consistency.

This profile is fairly similar to Marcos Molina's from several years ago. Molina's stuff just never came even most of the way back from a late-2015 Tommy John, even though the Mets gave him several extra years on the 40-man to get it together. He was ultimately released this past summer. Not all rehabs are alike, and not all rehabs are successful. We might not fully know where Szapucki is at until he steps back on a pro mound (hopefully) this spring. By this time next year, he could've reestablished No. 2 starter upside, or he could be a footnote.

The Risks: He hasn't thrown a competitive pitch since July 2017. In four pro seasons he's thrown 83⅓ innings, and only 29 in full-season ball. He's blown out his elbow already. He's had back problems already. He's had shoulder problems already. There's a lot going on here.

Bret Sayre's Fantasy Take: If you're going to gamble on a pitcher trying to return from an extended absence due to Tommy John, you at least want to bet on upside, and Szapucki still fits the bill here. The risk is sky-high, but a possible SP3 payoff with the ability to run up strikeouts still makes the southpaw worth holding onto in leagues that roster 250 prospects or more.

9. Anthony Kay   LHP
OFP: 50   Likely: 45   ETA: 2020
Born: 03/21/95   Age: 24   Bats: L   Throws: L   Height: 6'0"   Weight: 218
Origin: Round 1, 2016 Draft (#31 overall)

The Report: Kay was picked in the supplemental round in 2016 as a polished, quick to the majors, but relatively low-ceiling lefty. A UCL tear discovered shortly after the draft cost him six figures off his bonus and the 2017 season. The Mets—being the Mets—took it slowly with Kay in 2018, leaving him in the two full-season A-ball levels all year. The top line performance is fine and the stuff is most of the way back, and he still projects as a back-of-the-rotation three-pitch lefty.

The fastball sits in the low-90s from a tough angle with run and sink, and Kay will reach back for 95 on occasion. His breaking ball is an upper-70s curve that flashes tight 1-7 action, but he doesn't have consistent feel for it. The change was his party piece at UCONN, a potential plus offering, but it was too firm too often in his minor league debut. The hope is the stuff and command will tighten up a bit as he gets further removed from Tommy John surgery, but the whole moving fast thing hasn't happened, and Kay will be 24 in the spring.

The Risks: Medium. Kay was drafted as a fast-moving pitching prospect, but he's developmentally behind now and still hasn't seen the upper minors. We also don't know what the stuff will look like post-TJ.

Bret Sayre's Fantasy Take: A low-upside starting pitcher still recovering from a torn UCL? Sign me up.

10 **Simeon Woods-Richardson RHP** OFP: 55 Likely: 40 ETA: 2023
Born: 09/27/00 Age: 18 Bats: R Throws: R Height: 6'3" Weight: 210
Origin: Round 2, 2018 Draft (#48 overall)

The Report: One of my favorite 2018 draft stories—and an extremely Mets story—was that Simeon Woods-Richardson himself wasn't even expecting to get picked Day One. His velocity popped right before the draft though, and the Mets went overslot to buy him out of his commitment to the Longhorns.

Woods-Richardson dialed it up into the upper-90s in his pro debut after sitting more low-90s for most of high school, with a potential above-average breaker, and a delivery that has relief markers. He was young for his prep class, but is not particularly projectable by Texas prep arm standards. So for now he's an arm strength guy worth keeping an eye on, but he's already more intriguing than that pre-draft Day Two projection.

The Risks: Extreme. Eighteen-year-old arm strength and development bet. This can go several different ways.

Bret Sayre's Fantasy Take: Pro debuts deserve life-sized grains of salt, but SWR (let's save some space here, shall we) impressed enough prior to his 18th birthday to make him a reasonable late-round flier in dynasty drafts this offseason. That said, he's forever away, he's a pitcher, and the ceiling isn't obnoxiously high.

The Next Five:

11 **Jordan Humphreys RHP**
Born: 06/11/96 Age: 23 Bats: R Throws: R Height: 6'2" Weight: 223
Origin: Round 18, 2015 Draft (#539 overall)

Go back and read the Thomas Szapucki blurb, then mentally adjust it to a righty with a slightly worse breaking ball. Humphreys was one of early-2017's best breakout pitchers, suddenly showing three above-average pitches with command. Far too often, a bump in stuff like this is immediately followed by a blown elbow, and sure enough, Humphreys went down that summer. Like

Szapucki, he was conservatively held back for the entire 2018 season and we aren't going to know much here until we see him in a competitive game environment again. If healthy, he has mid-rotation upside and could move fast.

12 Tomas Nido   C
Born: 04/12/94   Age: 25   Bats: R   Throws: R   Height: 6'0"   Weight: 210
Origin: Round 8, 2012 Draft (#260 overall)

Last year, we thought Nido's defense and bat control would carry the day, despite weak offensive production at Double-A. After a 2018 repeat only went marginally better for the former Florida State League batting champion, Nido's bat now looks more like a backup's than a guy you want to give 400 plate appearances. He'll play anyway, because there's an extreme paucity of decent catching floating around these days. I suppose if you want to be kind, you can say he's likely to be above useless with the stick. But he appears on course to be the umpteenth straight promising Mets catching prospect who tops out well below his projection. Catchers are weird, man.

13 Junior Santos   RHP
Born: 08/16/01   Age: 17   Bats: R   Throws: R   Height: 6'8"   Weight: 218
Origin: International Free Agent, 2018

I'll confess that I am more comfortable making strange calls on the Mets list than most others. This is a particularly good year to do it since functionally this system is now 11 guys and then a Choose Your Own Adventure novel. Sometimes picking the 17-year-old projection bet sets you up to fall in an active volcano, but Santos has advanced stuff and control for a dude who spent most of the 2018 season only eligible for a learner's permit (and ineligible to pitch stateside). He'll flash three pitches, will touch 95, and is a—let's say—very projectable 6-foot-8. The Mets have generally done well with these low six-figures arms with some present feel for pitching. Santos might be nowhere near this list next year, or he might be near the top of it. I'd rather take a chance here than write another bland report on a major-league-ready reliever or Day 2 college pick.

14 Eric Hanhold   RHP
Born: 11/01/93   Age: 25   Bats: R   Throws: R   Height: 6'5"   Weight: 220
Origin: Round 6, 2015 Draft (#181 overall)

Hanhold could be Drew Smith, or Walter Lockett, or Kyle Dowdy, or any other fringy, swingy, middle relievery right-handed arm the Mets have acquired through various means (mostly 2017 deadline deals) to plug an inventory hole in their upper minors bullpens over the last two seasons. You should be developing these kinds of arms internally and in bulk, but the Mets have not. They've already started to weed their way through the new stock, DFAing Jamie Callahan, shipping Gerson Bautista to the Mariners, and sending Bobby Wahl out to

Milwaukee. Hanhold is the best of the remaining bunch on the combination of merit and proximity. He has a little major league service time. He has premium fastball velocity and an above-average breaking ball. The variance on these profiles is so high, maybe it's Dowdy breaking out and soaking up middle innings in Citi by May, maybe it's none of them. And it's a problem for the organization that I am mentioning any of them on this prospect list, even if they'd be behind the teenaged bats below on my personal pref list.

15. Desmond Lindsay   OF
Born: 01/15/97 Age: 22 Bats: R Throws: R Height: 6'0" Weight: 200
Origin: Round 2, 2015 Draft (#53 overall)

The Mets 2015 second round pick has struggled with injuries throughout his pro career. It used to be that whenever he was on the field, the everyday centerfielder tools would pop and you could talk yourself into him for one more year. All he needed was to stay healthy and get reps. Lower body injuries aren't always chronic, right? His 90 games in 2018 were a professional best, but the tools look more muted now. A swing tweak led to positive reviews in the Arizona Fall League, but what can you really project as the end product now for a 22-year-old that struggles with swing-and-miss and has trouble staying on the field? Short-side platoon outfielder? Normally I'd add here that if I really was completely out on Lindsay—I've long been an advocate—he wouldn't even have slid on to the back of this list. But… well, he didn't until the Mets traded away four prospects. That said, the system is so shallow right now that if Lindsay does come out in 2019 and show an average hit/power combo and the ability to play center again, well, there's a *Godfather 3* quote about that.

Others of note:

Hansel Moreno, IF, Low-A Columbia

To be frank, most of this list could broadly be categorized as "low minors sleepers" given the dearth of upper minors prospects, but we'll add a couple more. Moreno is a toolsy guy with present rawness, but he's already 22-years-old and only in A-ball. The aforementioned tools may not play on the dirt. He's filling out and slowing down, and the hands and arm at shortstop are more solid-average than plus. The Mets tried him all over in the South Atlantic League, and he might fit best in center field. There's potential above-average power in the profile, and he's already tapping into some of it pull side. Moreno's approach is raw enough—and he's old enough—that he might not be more than emergency depth, but he's also weirdly still projectable given his cohort. In conclusion, Hansel Moreno is a land of contrasts.

Stanley Consuegra, OF, GCL Mets

Now if I wanted to make a different weird call at #15, it could have easily been Consuegra on a different day or in a different mood. He's the more traditional 17-year-old complex league hero bet. The Mets gave him $500,000 as part of their 2017 July 2nd class, and he has center field tools and big exit velos, if you are into that sort of thing. He's a premium athlete with a lot of physical projection left, so this is more like the first page of a Choose Your Own Adventure book. The risk of falling into the volcano at the end is still very high.

Jaylen Palmer, IF, GCL Mets
When the Mets aren't spending Day Three popping low-ceiling college performers, they like to mix in the odd overslot local prep. It doesn't get much more locavore than Palmer, whose high school is a ten minute jaunt up I-678 from Citi Field. The Mets have had about as much luck with these prep flyers as the Day Three college bats, but Palmer might be a hidden gem. He had a huge growth spurt in high school and now garners Shervyen Newton comps. He's less likely to stick on the dirt than Newton, profiling best in a corner outfield spot, but he may also have the tools to carry that profile. Check back in four years to see if Gary Cohen will be making references to Flushing's own Jaylen Palmer or if that will be the purview of Tim Heiman.

Top Talents 25 and Under (born 4/1/93 or later):

1. Amed Rosario
2. Edwin Diaz
3. Andres Gimenez
4. Pete Alonso
5. Ronny Mauricio
6. Robert Gsellman
7. Shervyen Newton
8. Mark Vientos
9. David Peterson
10. Dominic Smith

Rosario is, for the time being, still a Met. His performance in the majors has been more mediocre than great, but sometimes we forget that he's only a year-and-a-half off being our no. 2 prospect in baseball on the 2017 midseason top 50. The low bar at shortstop means that even with his weak DRC+ and FRAA numbers, he was still about three-quarters of a win above replacement last year. He's been rumored to be available in trade, because he'll return a superstar and Gimenez is coming quickly; Gimenez might be a better long-term fit at shortstop if not quite a better player overall. That reality also could also push Rosario off shortstop to center field or third base within the next season or two if he remains a Met.

Diaz ahead of the top prospects feels hot takey, but it's also pretty clear that he has more value than Gimenez or Alonso. You'd trade either of those guys for him straight up in a heartbeat, no? Put it another way—Diaz is a role 7, and that's higher than either Gimenez or Alonso's OFP. He's among the small handful of the best relievers in baseball, he doesn't turn 25 until nearly Opening Day, and he's got a pretty clean pro health record. It's okay to question whether the Mets were in a position to be trading for an elite closer, but he's a hell of a pitcher.

Mickey Callaway spent a lot of the spring and summer using Gsellman like he was an Andrew Miller-style durable relief ace. It went better than it did in 2017—his fastball and slider played up in short bursts as we expected they might, and he should be at least a good MLB reliever moving forward. But he looked gassed at various points in the season when used too heavily. Diaz's acquisition should push him into a more traditional setup role, and hopefully he'll be supplemented by further acquisitions in the pen to take some of the load off.

The unceremonious salary dump of Jay Bruce slightly reopens the window for Smith to re-establish himself as a regular. 2018 was rough, with mediocre performance at both the majors and Triple-A followed by a short and difficult stint in winter ball. Somewhat bizarrely, he spent 39 games puttering around in the outfield in a fashion all too familiar to those who remember the escapades of Lucas Duda. There's playing time available at first base until the Mets end the service time charade and call Alonso up, but even there Smith's path has roadblocks. The current situation with four MLB infielders currently projected to split 2B/SS/3B could easily spill over into first base too. Time is becoming Smith's enemy.

Several circumstances conspired to make this list fairly easy. Michael Conforto and Brandon Nimmo are both ineligible by less than a month, and Jeff McNeil was a couple weeks more of missed playing time away from the rare "on the Top Ten but not on the 25U" exacta. Gsellman vs. Justin Dunn would've been a difficult call down here, but Dunn was gone before we had to make that choice. Drew Smith and Tyler Bashlor might've made a top 15, but they're clearly a cut below Kilome and Szapucki.

For the record, Jarred Kelenic would've ranked fourth before the trade, between Alonso and Mauricio. Dunn would've ranked fifth out of the prospects, between Mauricio and Newton. We'll have their full write-ups in the Seattle list, so long as the Mariners actually keep them.

Part 3: Featured Articles

The Hole in The Shift is Fixing Itself

Russell Carleton

I've been on a bit of a mission against The Shift of late. I'm not out to get The Shift for the usual reasons that people oppose it. The words "the right way to play the game" won't be found on my lips. If a team wants to pursue a strategy that is within the rules and it works, then by all means, they have my blessing (not that they need it). Instead, my concern with The Shift is a worry that it doesn't work, or at least that it has a flaw that needs fixing.

The data show that while The Shift does a decent job of preventing singles on balls in play (what it's supposed to do), it also increases the number of walks that happen in front of it, and the number of additional walks outweighs the number of singles saved. It's a problem because you can't throw a guy out if he gets to walk to first base.

But the "why" was important. It seemed that The Shift was changing the way in which pitchers pitched. We saw that there were fewer fastballs thrown in front of The Shift than we might otherwise expect, and that pitchers tended to stay out of the strike zone a little more. Not by a lot. In fact, it might not even be visible to the naked eye. The percentage of pitches that are out of the zone goes from 51.0 to 53.3 from a standard defense (two right/two left) to a full shift (three on one side). That difference stands up even after we control for the types of hitters that get shifted against. And it's enough to drive up the walk rate to where it cancels out the benefits that teams thought they were getting with The Shift... and then some.

But there was some hope. I found that when individual pitchers stayed closer to the in-zone/out-of-zone mix that they used without The Shift on, they could still get the benefits of The Shift without the walk problems. So, in theory, a team could simply figure out a way to convince its pitchers to not fall prey to the walk trap and The Shift would once again be their friend.

It's reasonable to think that some teams might be more hip to this idea than others. Maybe some figured it out a year before the others. Maybe they were better at getting the message across to their pitchers. Or, maybe no one has figured it out yet.

Warning! Gory Mathematical Details Ahead!

I used data from 2015-2017, made available through MLB's data portal, Baseball Savant. They are kind enough to note when teams are using an infield shift (three fielders on one side of second base), as opposed to a "strategic shift" (someone's playing a bit out of position, but it's not quite that drastic) or a "standard" alignment.

Since we're doing this by team, I can't just look at raw walk rates, because we know that some teams have good pitchers and others have not-so-good pitchers. Some have a mix of both. I used the log-odds ratio method to take into account a batter's general walking proclivities, and a pitcher's as well, and then shoving them into a binary logistic regression. Then, I asked the computer to generate a specific coefficient for each team's pitchers, for when they went into The Shift and how that affected their walk rate.

Using those coefficients, I was able to project what would happen if a league-average pitcher faced a league-average hitter (which we expect would produce a league-average walk rate; from 2015-2017, 7.7 percent of plate appearances ended in a walk) and then just switched his hat. Here's the top five and the bottom five:

Top 5 Teams	Projected Shift Walk Rate	Bottom 5 Teams	Projected Shift Walk Rate
Rockies	6.2%	Rangers	11.2%
Pirates	6.7%	Mets	10.4%
Indians	7.2%	Dodgers	10.2%
Astros	7.3%	Cardinals	9.9%
Braves	7.7%	Tigers	9.7%

There are probably people out there right now trying to figure out what the common thread is among the top and bottom teams. I'm sure, because this is Baseball Prospectus, people are already trying to make the case that sabermetric "early adopters" have some sort of edge here. I think that the more interesting piece is that by the time you get to fifth place in The Shift, we're at league average.

As a sanity check, I examined the issue on a pitch-by-pitch level, looking at how often pitchers threw their pitches in the GameDay strike zone, and again using the same basic methodology and getting team-specific coefficients. The names on the list re-arranged themselves, but the idea was the same, and the two lists correlated with an R of .593.

There's a reason that I don't usually do this type of leaderboard post. I don't really know what the Rockies, Pirates, Indians, Astros, and Braves have in common, or what they have that the bottom five don't. I can put a shrug emoji here and say, "Well, it must be something!" but that seems like a cop-out. Instead, I'd like to present another table and suggest that the table above doesn't even really matter anymore.

Year	League Percent Outside K Zone (Full Shift)	League Percent in K Zone (No Shift)	Difference
2015	54.1%	51.1%	3.0%
2016	53.3%	50.9%	2.4%
2017	52.6%	50.9%	1.7%
2018	52.0%	50.7%	1.3%

The hole in The Shift is fixing itself, and it's coming down really fast league wide. In my earlier work on The Shift, I suggested that until teams stopped having such a huge difference between their out-of-zone rate with and without The Shift on, there would just be too many walks for The Shift to make sense. It seems that all 30 of them have been working toward just that. I once estimated that it takes about 10 years for an idea to filter its way through baseball. At this rate, it looks like teams are going to catch up a lot faster than that. And yeah, they're all saber-smart now.

It's likely that whatever magic it was that the Rockies and Pirates had has made its way to Texas and Queens. Or is at least on its way. And if teams are committing to fixing the walk problem, then it's likely that they will continue shifting and shifting a lot.

And eventually it's going to actually make sense for them to do it.

—Russell Carleton is a former author of Baseball Prospectus and now an analyst for the New York Mets.

The State of the Quality Start

Rob Mains

One of the seven things you (probably) didn't know about the 2018 season is that quality starts—defined as a start lasting six or more innings with three or fewer earned runs allowed—as a percentage of total starts cratered to an all-time low of 41 percent. I want to look a little more deeply into this, since it's been a while (May of 2016, to be exact) since I've examined quality starts.

The term *quality start* is credited to *Philadelphia Inquirer* sportswriter John Lowe. It's been derided ever since he coined it in December of 1985. Three runs in six innings? That's a 4.50 ERA! In what world is that a measure of quality?

Let's start with that criticism. It's true that 3 x 9 / 6 = 4.5. (You came here for this sort of high-level math, right?) But it's also true that type of start, meeting the bare minimum for earning a quality start, is unusual. Here's the proportion of quality starts in which the pitcher lasted exactly six innings and yielded exactly three earned runs. (I'm going to confine this analysis to the 30-team era, 1998-present. Almost all data retrieved in this article is via the Baseball-Reference Play Index.)

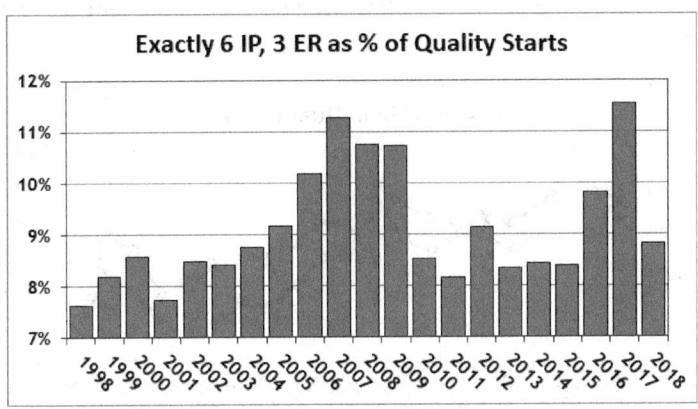

There were 1,997 quality starts in 2018. Only 176, or fewer than one in 11, featured a pitcher going six innings and allowing three earned runs. Put another way, the percentage of quality starts that resulted in a 4.50 ERA (8.8 percent) is less than half the percentage of games in which a batter hit two home runs and his team lost (22.5 percent; 237-69 won-lost). That doesn't impugn hitting two homers.

So if a 4.50 ERA isn't the norm, what is? How good are quality starts?

Pretty good, it turns out. First, on a team level:

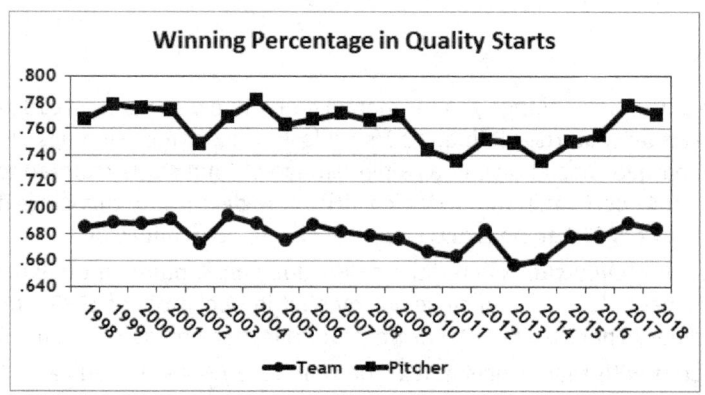

Teams receiving a quality start from their pitcher won 68.4 percent of their games in 2018, in line with the 30-team era average of 67.9 percent. A team with a .684 winning percentage wins 111 games. Getting a quality start is definitely a good thing. Individual pitchers throwing quality starts have a higher winning percentage because a big slice of team losses is assigned to a reliever.

If teams do well in quality starts, how well do the starting pitchers do? Again, very well.

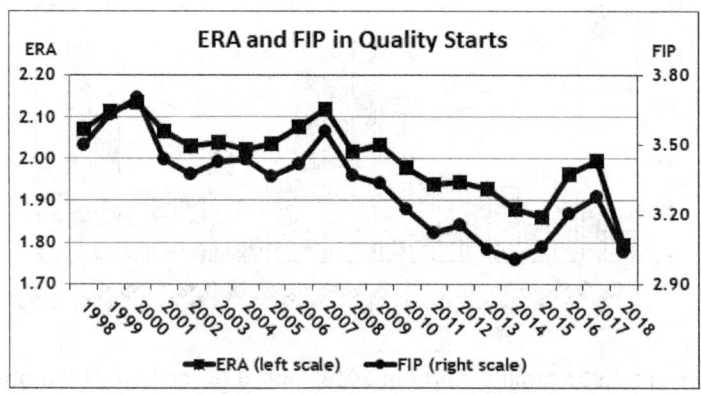

Pitchers in quality starts had a 1.79 ERA (blue line) in 2018, *the lowest in the 30-team era*. Their FIP was higher, 3.04, but still excellent. In the 30-team era, only 2014 had a lower FIP for quality starts, 3.01.

But, of course, the run environment in 2014 was different. Teams in 2014 scored 4.07 runs per game, the fewest in a non-strike year since 1976. They scored 4.45 runs per game in 2018. So surrendering a 3.04 FIP in 2018 is more impressive than 3.01 in 2014. Accordingly, let's look at ERA and FIP in quality starts relative to league averages.

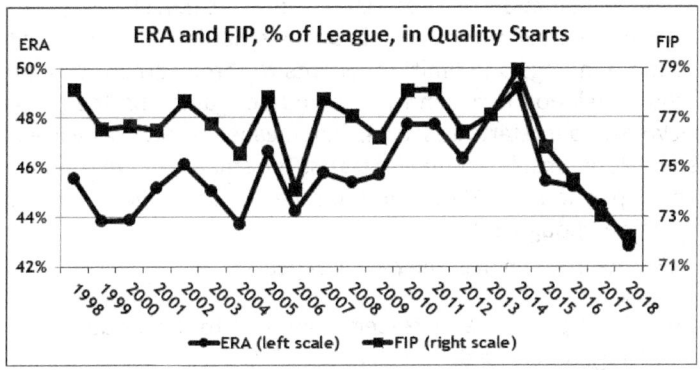

This tells a more dramatic story. Starting pitchers in 2018 gave up a 4.19 ERA and a 4.21 FIP. Starters in quality starts gave up a 1.79 ERA, 43 percent of the league average. Starters in quality starts gave up a 3.04 FIP, 72 percent of the league average. Both of these marks represent lows in the 30-team era.

The takeaway here is this: *Quality starts are better, relative to other starts, than they've ever been over the past 21 years.*

Maybe during the winter I'll look at this over a longer arc of time. For now, though, we can definitively say quality starts are the best they've ever been since the Diamondbacks and Rays joined the majors.

Yet, paradoxically, they're down.

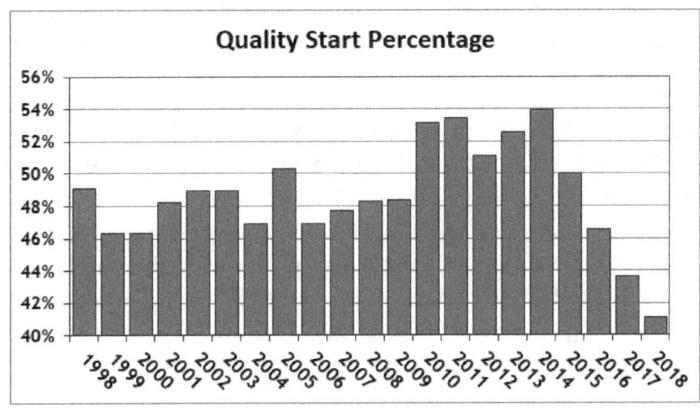

The State of the Quality Start - 127

This graph covers only the 30-team era. In my article last week, though, I looked at the years 1908-2018. The result was the same. The 41 percent of starts in 2018 that were quality starts are an all-time low, well below the runners-up: 1930's 43 percent (the year teams scored an all-time record 5.55 runs per game) and last year's 44 percent.

The normal explanation for a dip in quality start percentage is an increase in scoring. When teams score a lot of runs, it's harder for starting pitchers to last six or more innings and limit opponents to three earned runs. From 1998 to 2014, the correlation between runs scored per game and the percentage of starts that were quality starts was -0.94. That means there was an extremely close relationship: More runs, fewer quality starts. Too small a sample? Go back to the start of the Expansion Era, 1961, and the relationship is even more negative, a -0.95 correlation, though 2014.

But that's broken down over the past four years:

- 2015: Runs per game increased from 4.07 to 4.25, quality start percentage decreased from 54.0 to 50.1. Yes, that's a negative relationship, but the regression model would predict a decline of 1.5 percentage points. We got 3.9 instead.
- 2016: Runs per game increased from 4.25 to 4.48, quality start percentage decreased from 50.1 to 46.6. Past experience would suggest a decline of just 1.8 percentage points. We got 3.4.
- 2017: Runs per game increased from 4.48 to 4.65, quality start percentage decreased from 46.6 to 43.6. Again, the direction's right, but the magnitude isn't. Using the relationship from 1998 to 2014, that increase in scoring should've reduced quality starts by 1.3 percentage points, not 2.9.
- 2018: Runs per game declined from 4.65 to 4.45. That should've resulted in the quality start percentage moving in the other direction, rising 1.6 points. It didn't. It fell 2.6 points, as noted, to an all-time low.

Granted, we're talking about just four years here. Maybe they're outliers. But I don't think they are. Quality starts, as noted, are as good or better than ever. But they're rarer than ever as well. And I think I know why.

To get a quality start, you need to allow three or fewer earned and pitch at least six innings. That's 18 outs. Here's a graph showing the number of starting pitchers who limited their opponents to three or fewer earned runs but got pulled after pitching at least five innings but fewer than six:

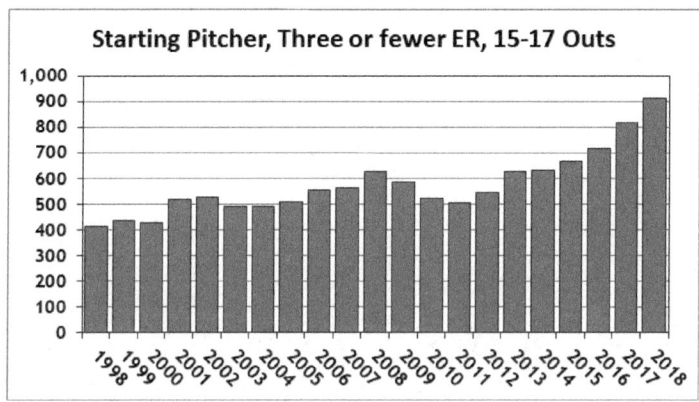

A pitcher getting 15 outs pitched five innings. A pitcher getting 16 outs pitched 5 1/3. A pitcher getting 17 outs pitched 5 2/3. More than ever before, pitchers are being removed from games in which they are within 1-3 outs of a quality start, falling just short of the six-inning finish line. Widespread acknowledgement of the times-through-the-order penalty and a flotilla of available bullpen arms is making the quality start simultaneously both more excellent and more rare.

Which is ironic, given that we saw a new post-war quality start record this season:

Rank	Pitcher	Season	Consecutive QS
1	Jacob deGrom	2018	24
2	Bob Gibson	1968	22
-	Chris Carpenter	2005	22
4	Johan Santana	2004	21
5	Luis Tiant	1968	20
-	Mike Scott	1986	20
-	Jake Arrieta	2015	20
8	Robin Roberts	1952	19
-	Tom Seaver	1973	19
-	Jack Morris	1983	19
-	Greg Maddux	1998	19
-	Josh Johnson	2010	19
-	Jon Lester	2014	19

While there have been longer streaks spread over multiple seasons, no pitcher since World War II threw more consecutive quality starts in one year than Jacob deGrom this year. The fact that he did in a year in which quality starts were the rarest they've ever been adds to the accomplishment.

—*Rob Mains is an author of Baseball Prospectus.*

Heads-Up Hacking—The First Pitch

Matthew Trueblood

Batters fell behind in a higher percentage of all plate appearances in 2018 than in any previous season for which we have pitch-by-pitch data. That kind of granular information goes back only to 1988, but we might safely assume (given all we know about baseball as it had been before that, and as it has been in the years since) that batters have *never* fallen behind at a higher rate than they did last season.

Through the 1990s, the percentage of all plate appearances that began 0-1 hovered in the high 30s and low 40s. In the 2000s, it rose steadily but slowly, through the mid-40s. In 2018, 49.8 percent of all trips to the plate began 0-1. That, as much as anything, captures in microcosm the nature of hitting in MLB today.

A countdown clock toward strike three begins ticking almost the moment a batter takes his place in the box. The league's adjusted OPS+ on the first pitch was higher in 2018 than ever before, and that has been true in most of the last 10 seasons. Batters hit .264/.289/.442 in all plate appearances in which they swung at the first pitch last season, and .241/.330/.395 in all plate appearances in which they took that first offering.

The percentage differences in batting average and isolated power there favor swinging at the first pitch by more than in any season since 1988, while the difference in on-base percentage favors taking by more than ever. If you want to get on base at a decent clip, it's a good idea to be patient, but you run the risk of missing the only chances you'll get to produce power.

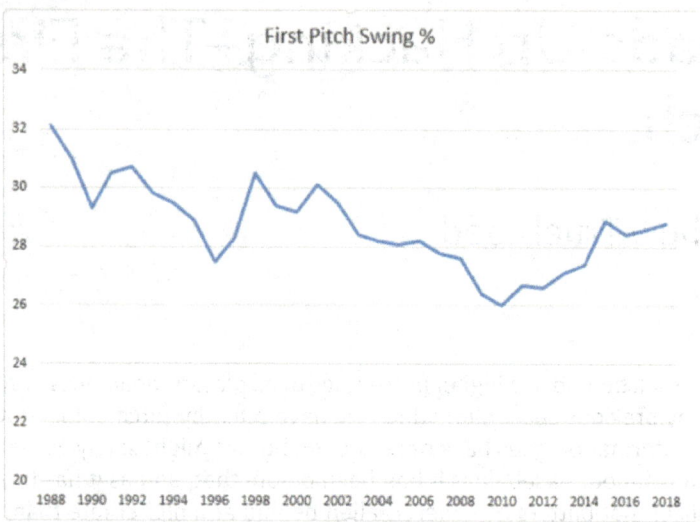

The league swung at the first pitch 28.8 percent of the time in 2018. With the isolated exception of 2015, that's the highest that number has climbed since 2002, but it might not be high enough. With the help of BP research maven Rob McQuown, I looked at the aggregate Called Strike Probability (CSProb) on the first pitch for each season since 2008, when the implementation of PITCHf/x first made measuring that possible. It's risen sharply during that period.

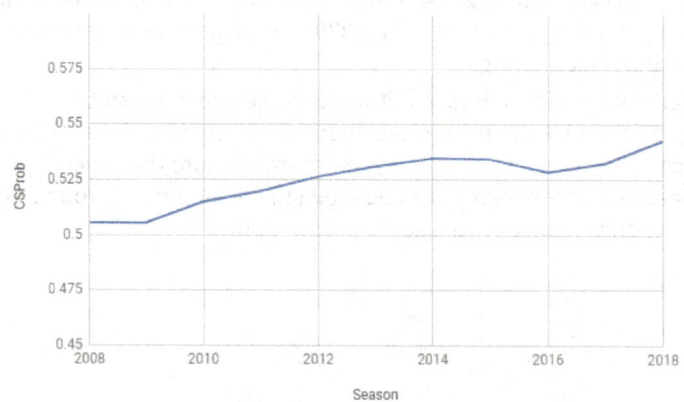

Called Strike Probability, First Pitch of PA (2008-2018)

Called Strike Probability is exactly what it sounds like: a pitch with a given CSProb has roughly that chance of being called a strike, if not swung at. In 2018, a batter who took 100 first pitches from a random sampling of the league's pitchers might expect to fall behind 54 or 55 times—up from 50 or 51 times in 2008. Almost regardless of pitch type (and, notably, especially in the case of fastballs), the first pitch tends to have more of the zone right now than ever before.

Pitchers are better at throwing strikes. They have better stuff, and believe more in their ability to miss bats within the zone. Perhaps most importantly, they know that batters are looking for one thing on the first pitch: a fastball. If they don't get it, they're likely to take the pitch. Check out how the use of sinkers and four-seamers on the first pitch has changed in a decade:

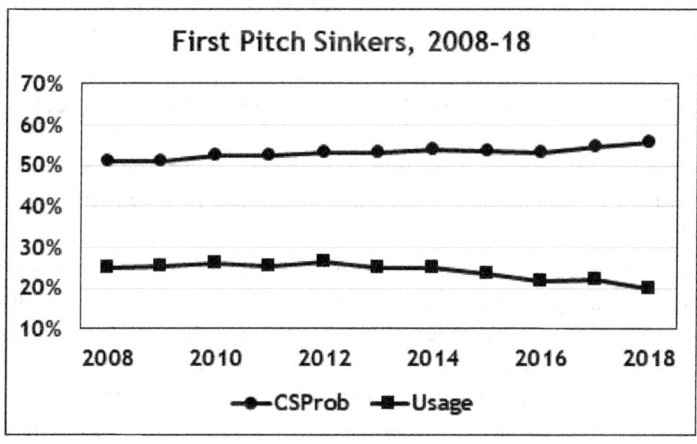

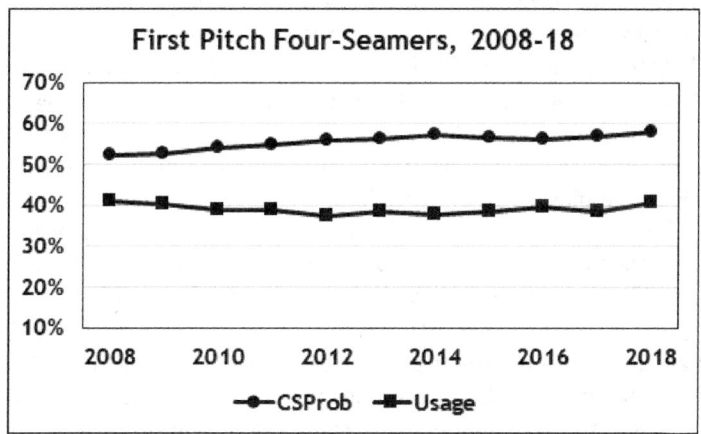

The sinker is losing its place in baseball, but the rate at which pitchers have thrown it on the first pitch hasn't dropped any faster than its usage rate in other counts. Pitchers have actually gone to their four-seamer *more* often to open counts, in the last few years, after a dip in the 2012-2015 period. What's really changed, though, and what shows up in both charts above, is that pitchers are catching more of the zone with first-pitch fastballs than they were a decade ago, or a half-decade ago. They're attacking right away, even with the pitch they know batters are expecting. The message is pretty clear: batters are being too passive.

Sliders, curves, and changeups each have more of the zone when thrown on the first pitch than they did several years ago, too, though the effect is less pronounced. Pitchers have seen the numbers; they know batters are doing better on the first pitch itself. They still feel safe throwing more and better strikes than ever before, figuring they'll come out ahead as long as they keep getting ahead to open each battle.

The Moneyball revolution brought an increased league-wide focus on OBP, which resulted in a de facto mandate to take a more patient tack at the plate. It worked very well for a while, as batters with poor plate discipline were compelled to either adjust or be expelled from the league, and pitchers with poor control were slowly weeded out.

However, concurrent with that revolution, and spurred by it in some ways, was the evolution of the pitching paradigm that now dominates the game. As batters ratcheted up their focus on inflating pitch counts and working walks, pitchers honed theirs on throwing strikes and missing bats. The league's understanding of what makes a good pitcher improved at least as much, from the mid-1990s through the mid-2000s, as its understanding of what makes a good hitter. As amphetamines and other performance-enhancing drugs were phased mostly out of the game, and as PITCHf/x broke onto the scene, individuals and teams learned how to exploit the evolved approaches of even the smartest hitters.

The ability to avoid making outs is still the most valuable one in baseball, but the magnitude of its eclipse of slugging is smaller than ever. To a greater extent than power, on-base skills derive their value from chaining—from the on-base skill levels of the players on either side of a given individual. Eleven years ago, when the housing crisis hit, people learned the hard way that the value of their homes depended a good deal on the values of their neighbors' homes. The same wasn't true, though, of their cars. So it is now, with OBP and SLG.

The global OBP in 2018 was .318. The only seasons since the Dead Ball Era in which the league got on base at a worse clip were 2013-2015, 1988, 1971-1972, and 1963-1968. This is all happening despite the aforementioned evolution of the science of hitting. It's happening despite a shift in approach and focus, one that would steer OBP ever higher, if only it were working.

Instead, it's sitting at a low ebb, and while it does so, even guys who get on base often are a little less helpful than they were 10 years ago—or 20, or 40, or 60, or 70, or 80, or 90. They're less helpful, that is, because unless there happen to be three or four other guys in the lineup who get on just as regularly, their contribution is merely to forestall the inevitable. Runs happen, increasingly, when a sudden bang happens, and that means attacking early in the count—because pitchers are sure as hell doing that.

In a league making contact on barely 75 percent of its swings, and a league in which an increasing number of pitchers can throw multiple off-speed pitches for strikes in any count, the only way to consistently generate offense is going to be aggressive. This isn't necessarily true for individuals, like Mookie Betts and Jose Ramirez, who make a lot of contact and have excellent plate discipline, and whose power comes from such natural quickness in a short stroke. Most players have to make tradeoffs, though, whether it be lowering their contact rate or raising their chase rate, in order to consistently make the quality of contact necessary to survive in today's game.

Highest %	Lowest %
Javier Baez – 48.3	Joe Mauer – 4.6
Freddie Freeman – 47.1	Mookie Betts – 9.7
Ozzie Albies – 46.3	Brett Gardner – 10.7
Jose Altuve – 44.2	Jose Ramirez – 12.0
Nick Castellanos – 44.1	Jason Kipnis – 13.8
Joey Gallo – 42.3	Jesus Aguilar – 14.5
Corey Dickerson – 40.9	Xander Bogaerts – 15.8
Salvador Perez – 40.8	Brian Dozier – 16.3
Eddie Rosario – 40.7	Mike Trout – 17.6
Nick Ahmed – 40.4	Yasmani Grandal – 17.6

Top 10 and Bottom 10 Hitters, First-Pitch Swing Rate (2018)

The question isn't which of these lists one prefers, but what they each convey, qualitatively, about the cat-and-mouse game of early-count hitting. Those top five on the left, especially, drive home the fact that for most players, getting aggressive early in the count is now key to keeping strikeout rate down and hitting for power.

For now, the message is: pitchers are coming right after batters with the nastiest stuff they've ever had. Batters had better stop giving away strike one and force hurlers to adjust, or the global OBP crisis is only going to get worse.

—*Matthew Trueblood is an author of Baseball Prospectus.*

A Hymn for the Index Stat

Patrick Dubuque

We survived without computers. I know this, because I remember the day when my dad hooked up his brand-new Atari 400 computer to the back of our 12-inch Magnavox television, and the perfect blue of the memo pad lit up for the first time. I was born just on the edge of that transitional generation, of learning cursive and balancing checkbooks and just doing math all the time, constant manual arithmetic.

It still amazes me. We learned how to sail ships without computers. We learned how to do calculus. We built towers that didn't fall down, most of the time. We engineered catapults to knock them down anyway. We built a robust system of philosophy called "utilitarianism," founded on the principle that the good of an action is evaluated by summing the effects of that action, which is the kind of formula that would make the world's mainframes crash. The whole foundation of statistics as a field is "here's math you could easily do but would die of old age first."

The fact of the matter is that there is too much math in the world to do. There are too many things changing, and too many things too small to notice, for us to handle. At some point, they become too much for the computers to handle as well, which is why we have chaos theory and undetectable earthquakes, but it's not an even fight. At some point, we fall back on intuition, and given how under-equipped we are, we're forced to bestow that intuition with some sort of supernatural superiority, the "gut feeling," that we can't prove because we can only intuit that our intuition is better.

We're all lousy at intuition, and wonderful at lying to ourselves about it. The honest truth is that computers are far better at intuition than we are, because in order to know what feels "off" you have to know what's "on." In order to do that you have to constantly reassess the average of everything, then re-rank your own experience against it.

Test your own, by comparing these three anonymous lines:

Player	G	HR	AVG	OBP	SLG
Player A	156	38	.259	.342	.535
Player B	154	38	.280	.348	.527
Player C	158	38	.266	.343	.509

These all seem like pretty similar players, right? The second one a touch more batted-ball dependent, the third a little less strong, but all pretty good hitters. And you'd be right, about the latter. Not the former.

Here's the breakdown:

- Player A: 1991 Howard Johnson, 141 DRC+
- Player B: 1996 Dean Palmer, 121 DRC+
- Player C: 2018 Giancarlo Stanton, 114 DRC+

Baseball is fortunate to have escaped the seismic shifts of so many other sports, where the talents and performances of other eras are nearly unrecognizable. (And not just other sports: try to explain the greatness of the movie Duck Soup without adjusting for era.) But they're still there, and they're nearly impossible to account for manually, without having to resort to sweeping generalizations like "steroid era" or juiced-ball era" to throw out entire swathes of production.

This is all to say that we should celebrate the index stat, that simple 100-based scale with such a humble aim: just to give context. It's hard to imagine how we lived without them for so long. Sabermetricians have always tried to make their stats look like other stats: True Average mapped to batting average, FIP molded to look like and compare to ERA. It's easy to understand the motivation—these statistics carry an emotional value in them that is hard to resist, as with the .300 hitter and the 2.00 ERA—but even they fall prey to the same loss of scale as their unadjusted counterparts. If a .300 average means different things in different years, does that hold true for a .300 True Average?

Instead, 100 doesn't say anything, except above average or below. And it does it instantly, for every season in every run environment for any statistic we want it to. We should have more index stats: K%+, so we can stop comparing Mike Clevinger's career 9.46 K/9 to Nolan Ryan's 9.55. HBP%+, so we can note that Ron Hunt was getting plunked when nobody else was getting plunked, as opposed to that imitator Brandon Guyer. Some might note how stale these references are and accuse league-adjustment as a backward-looking drive, and this is true. But we're always looking backward, always comparing the new with the expectations already set. The index stat just forces us to be honest.

There's always resistance to a new statistic, especially one so outwardly simple and so internally complex. We tend to stick with what we know, even in the case of formulas that are supposed to tell us what we know. But if your resistance is that it seems too complicated, too counterintuitive, too "black boxy," I encourage you to consider why you feel that way. Because the real world is infinitely more complicated than baseball, where all the pitches go in one basic direction and the baserunners are only allowed to travel in four directions. Baseball statistics based on mixed methodology are almost impossibly intricate. So are skyscrapers and automobiles. That's why we have computers—to take the guesswork out of them.

—*Patrick Dubuque is an author of Baseball Prospectus.*

Index of Names

Alonso, Pete 94, 108
Avilan, Luis 60
Bashlor, Tyler 62
Blanco, Gregor 103
Broxton, Keon 103
Cano, Robinson 22
Cecchini, Gavin 103
Cespedes, Yoenis 24
Conforto, Michael 26
Conlon, P.J. 104
Cortes, Carlos 103
d'Arnaud, Travis 95
Davis, J.D. 28
Davis, Rajai 30
deGrom, Jacob 64
Diaz, Edwin 66
Familia, Jeurys 68
Flexen, Chris 104
Frazier, Todd 32
Gagnon, Drew 70
Gimenez, Andres 96, 107
Gomez, Carlos 34
Gsellman, Robert 72
Guillorme, Luis 36
Hanhold, Eric 100, 115
Hechavarria, Adeiny 38
Herrera, Dilson 40
Humphreys, Jordan 114
Kay, Anthony 104, 113
Kilome, Franklyn 101, 112
Lagares, Juan 42
Lee, Braxton 103
Lindsay, Desmond 103, 116
Lockett, Walker 104
Lowrie, Jed 44
Lugo, Seth 74
Matz, Steven 76
Mauricio, Ronny 97, 109
McNeil, Jeff 46
Mesoraco, Devin 48
Newton, Shervyen 98, 110
Nido, Tomas 50, 115
Nimmo, Brandon 52
Oswalt, Corey 78
Peterson, David 102, 111
Peterson, Timothy 104
Ramos, Wilson 54
Rhame, Jacob 104
Rosario, Amed 56
Ryan, Ryder 104
Sanchez, Ali 103
Santiago, Hector 80
Santos, Junior 115
Sewald, Paul 82
Smith, Dominic 58
Smith, Drew 104
Syndergaard, Noah 84
Szapucki, Thomas 112
Tebow, Tim 103
Vargas, Jason 86
Vientos, Mark 99, 110
Villines, Stephen 104

New York Mets 2019

Wheeler, Zack 88
Wilson, Justin 90
Woods-Richardson, Simeon . 104, 114
Zamora, Daniel 92

Ballpark diagrams for Baseball Prospectus are created by THIRTY81Project, a design concept offering original ballpark artwork, including the new 'Ballparks of 2019' 11 x 17 color print.

Visit **www.thirty81project.com** for full details.

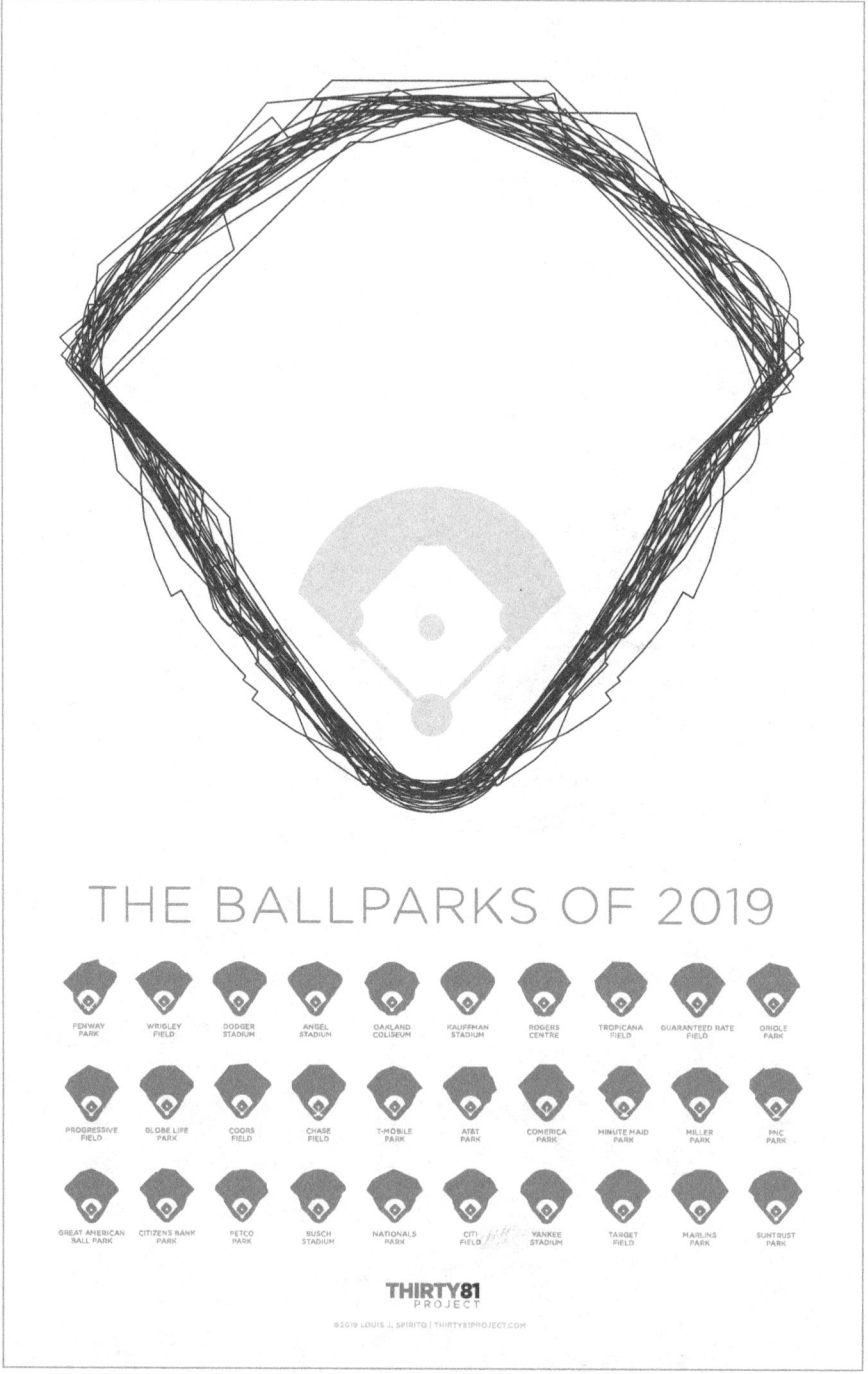